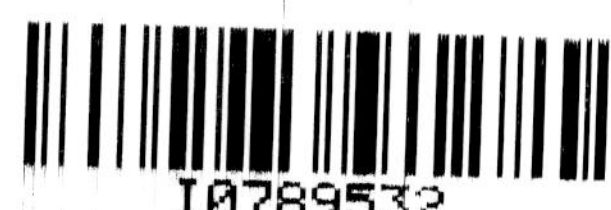

This book belong to :

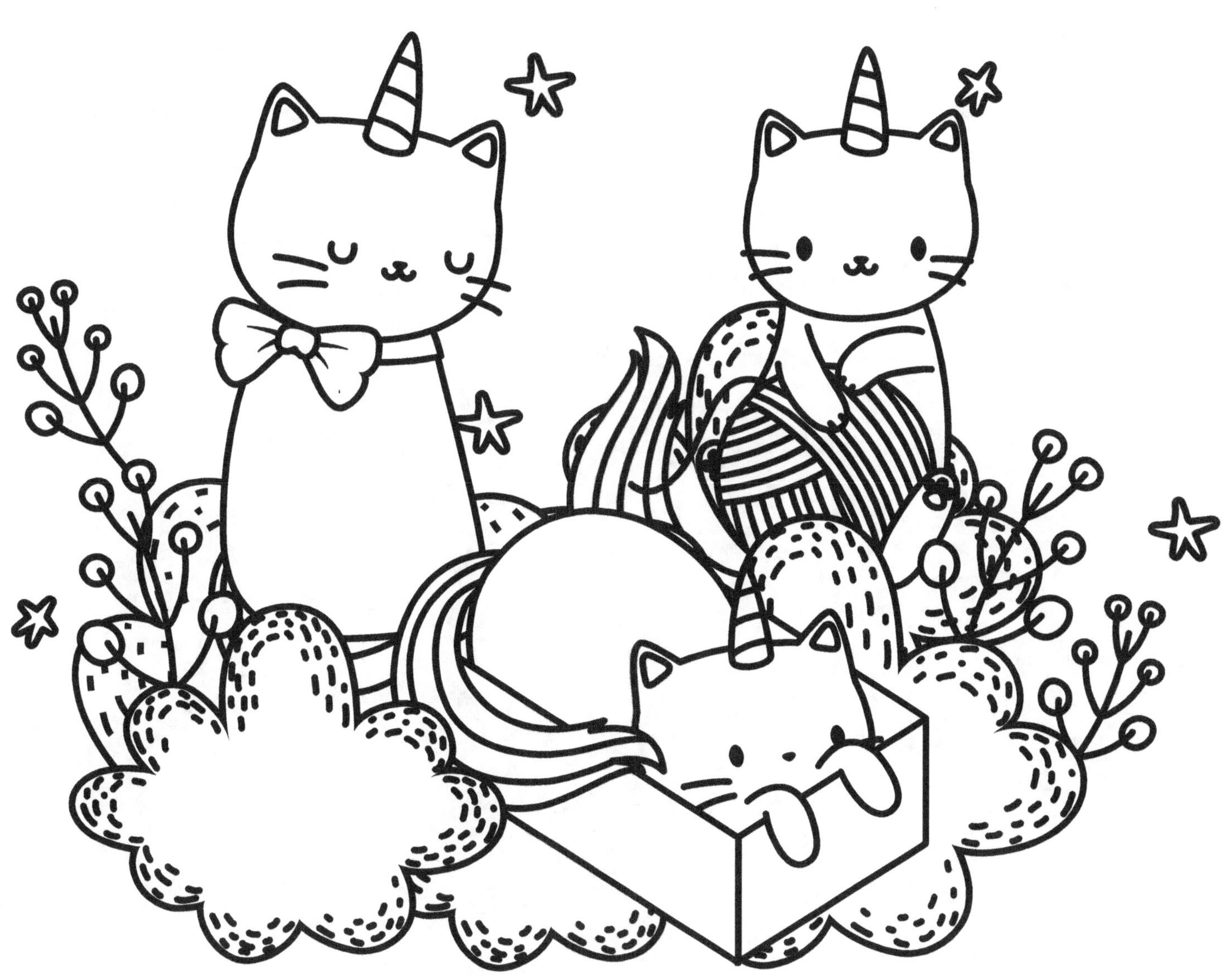

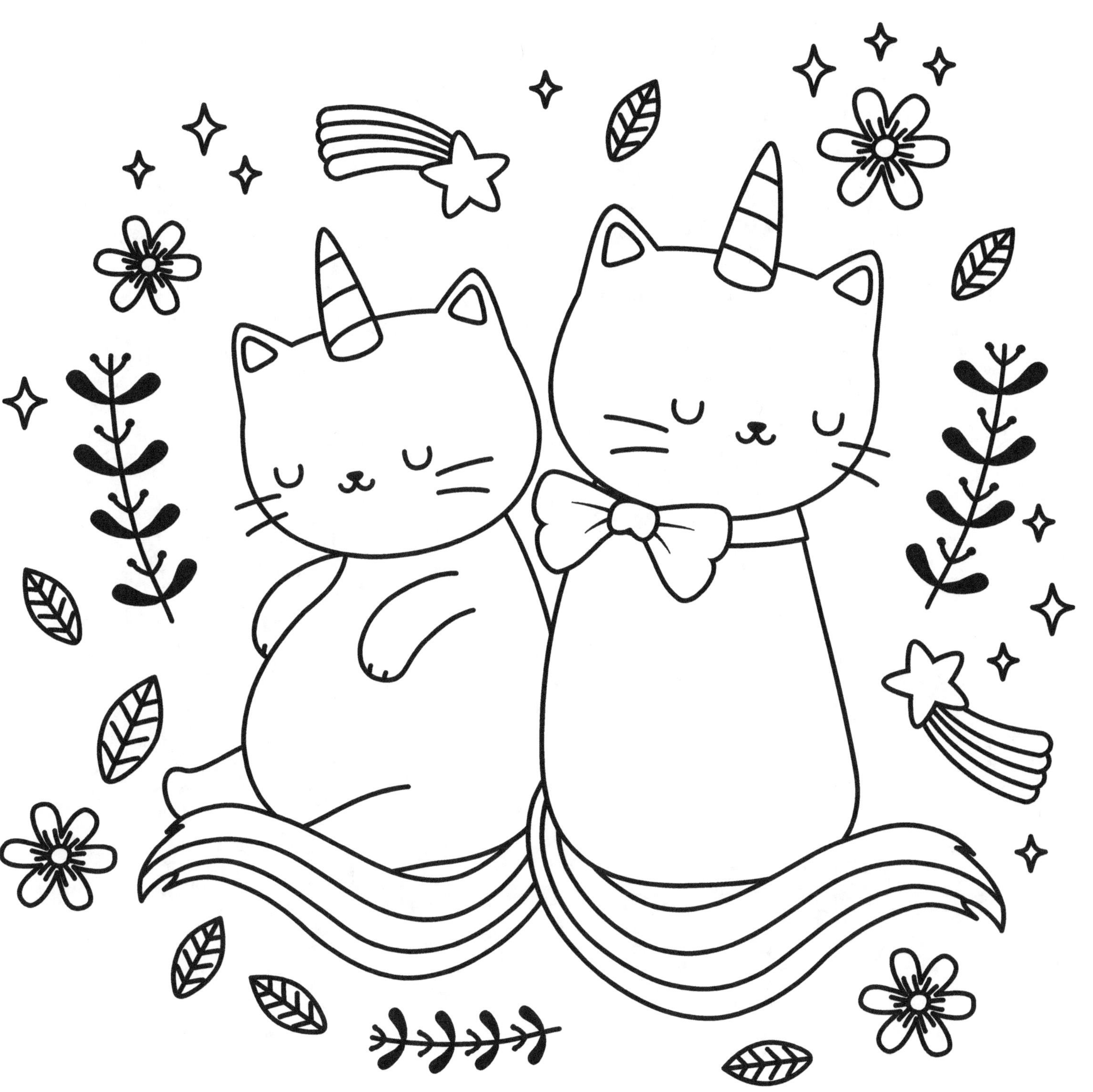

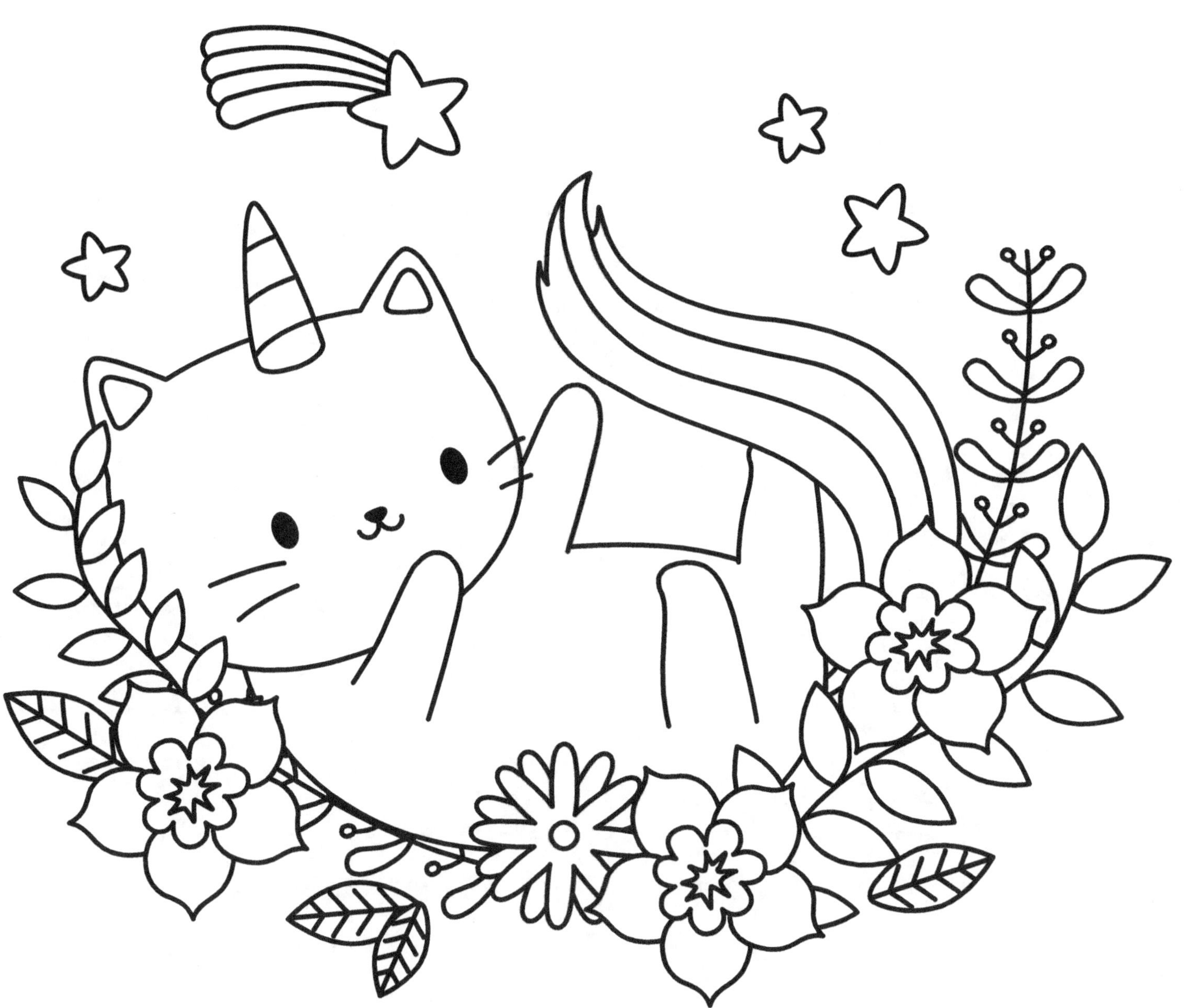

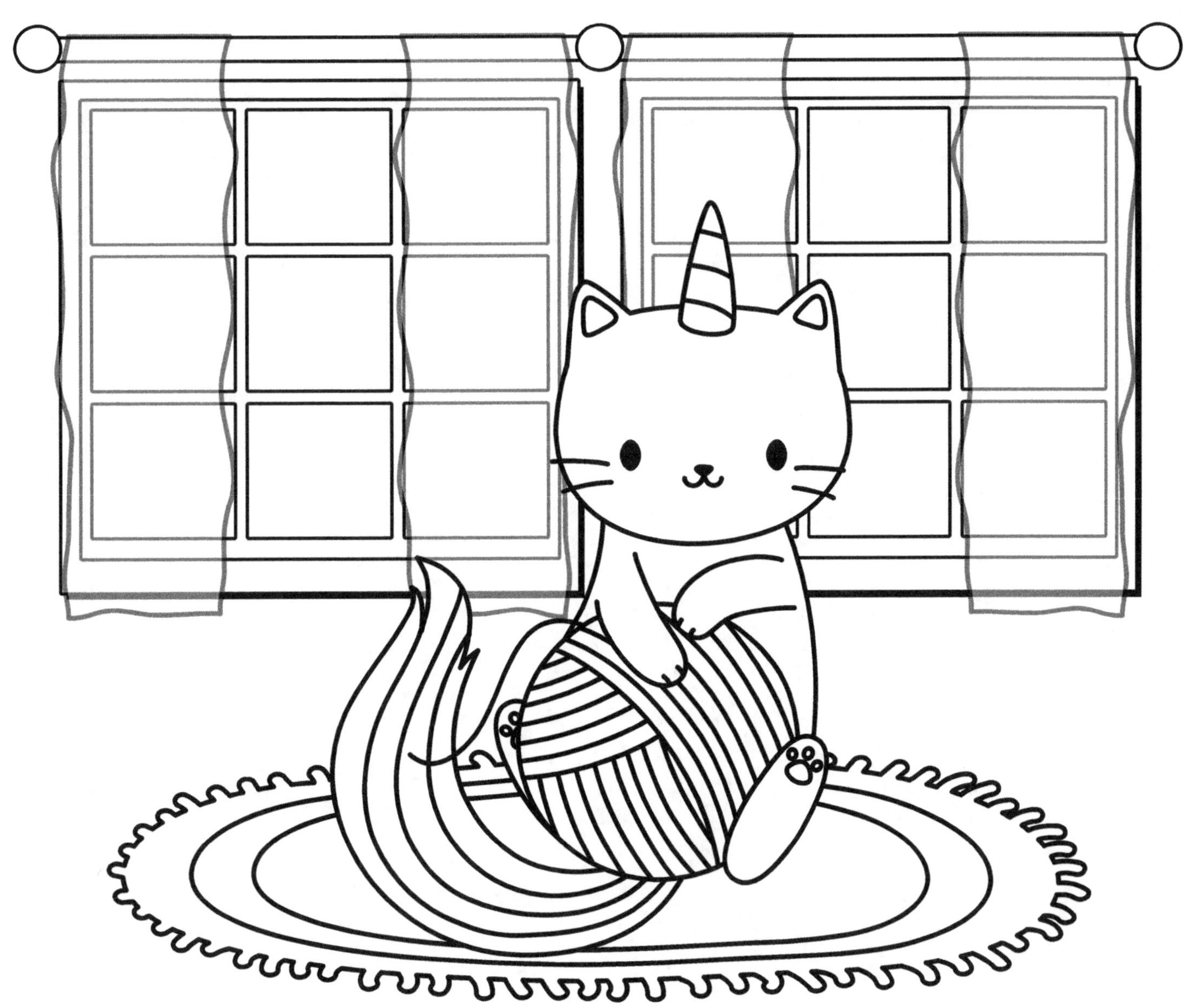

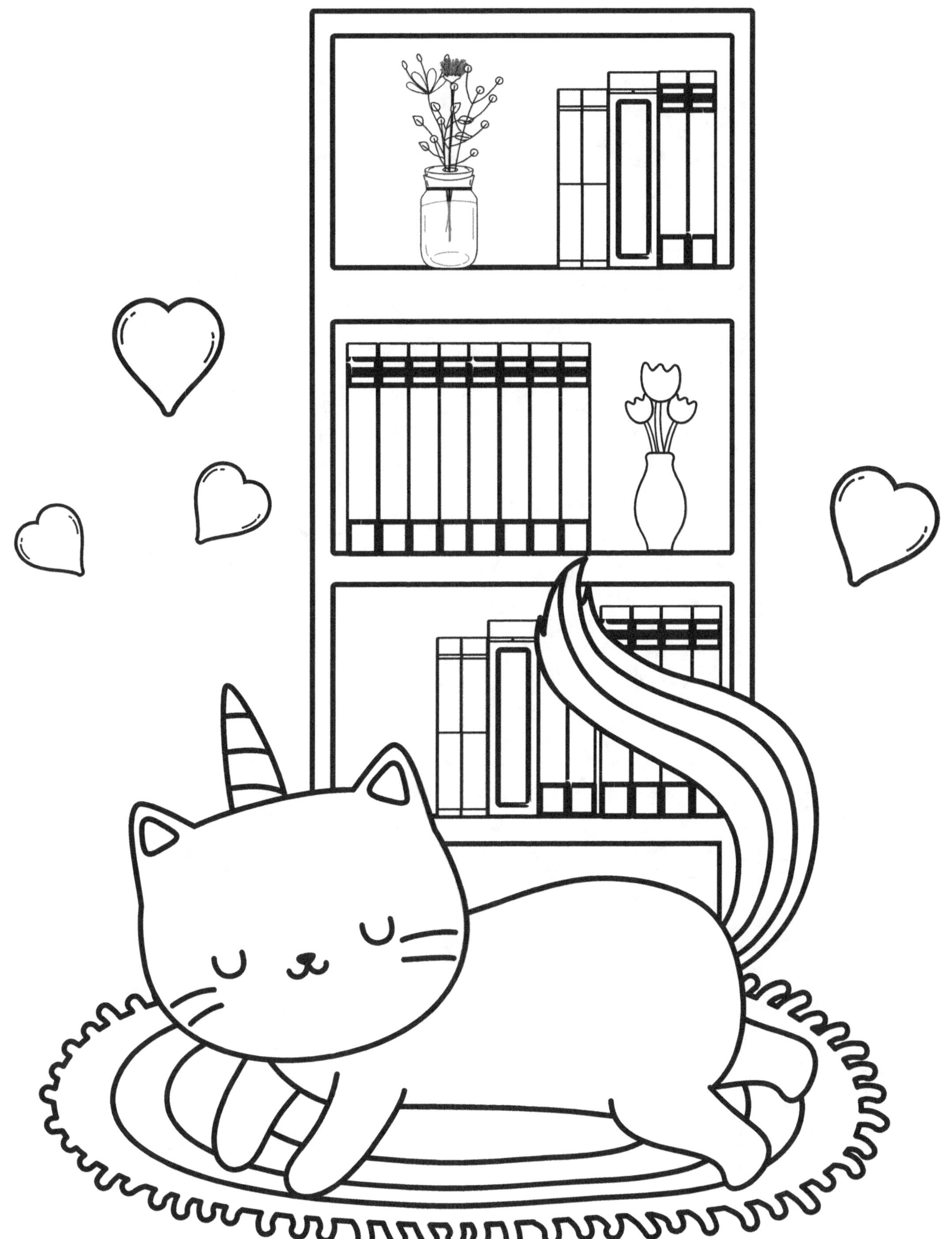

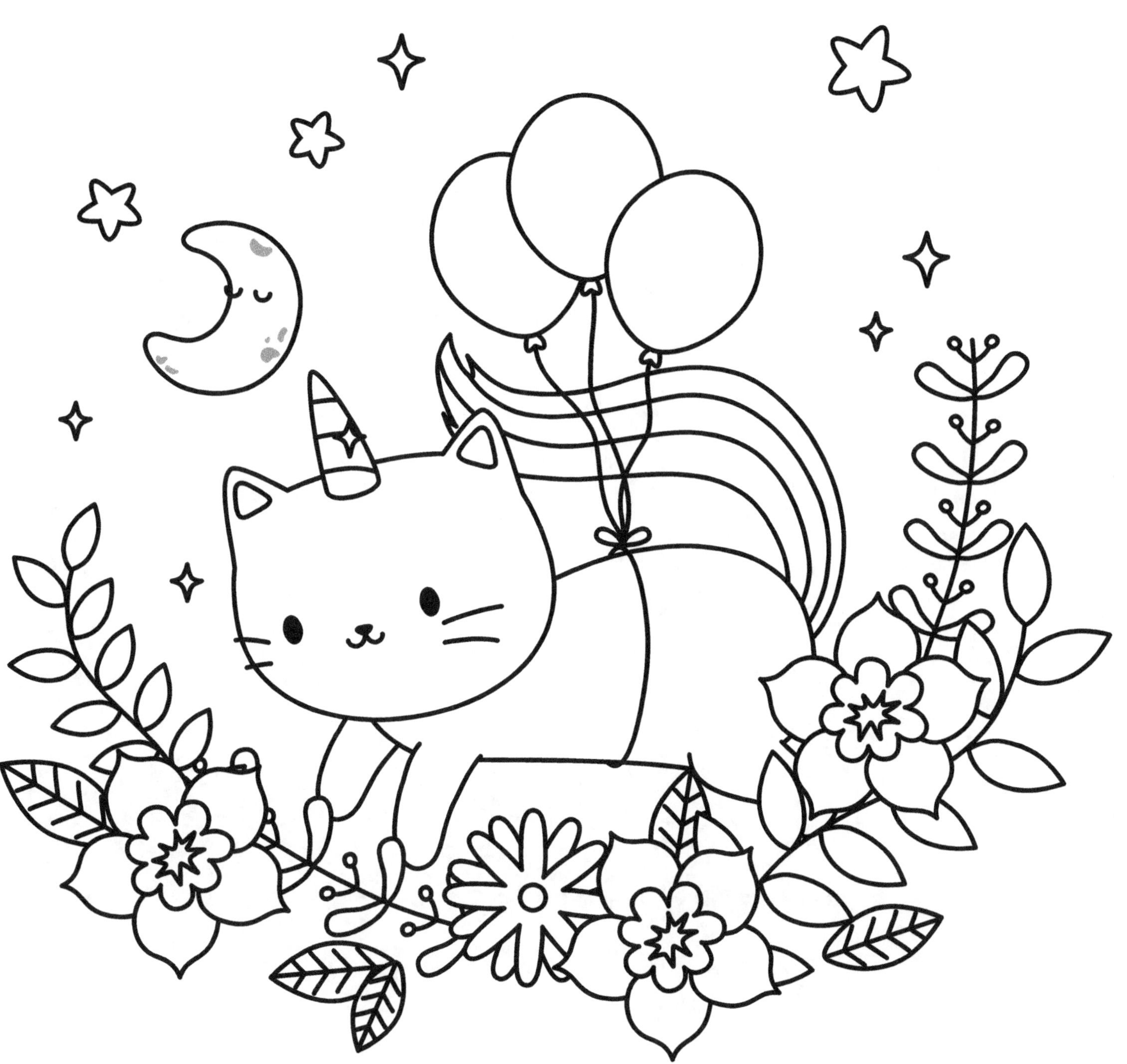

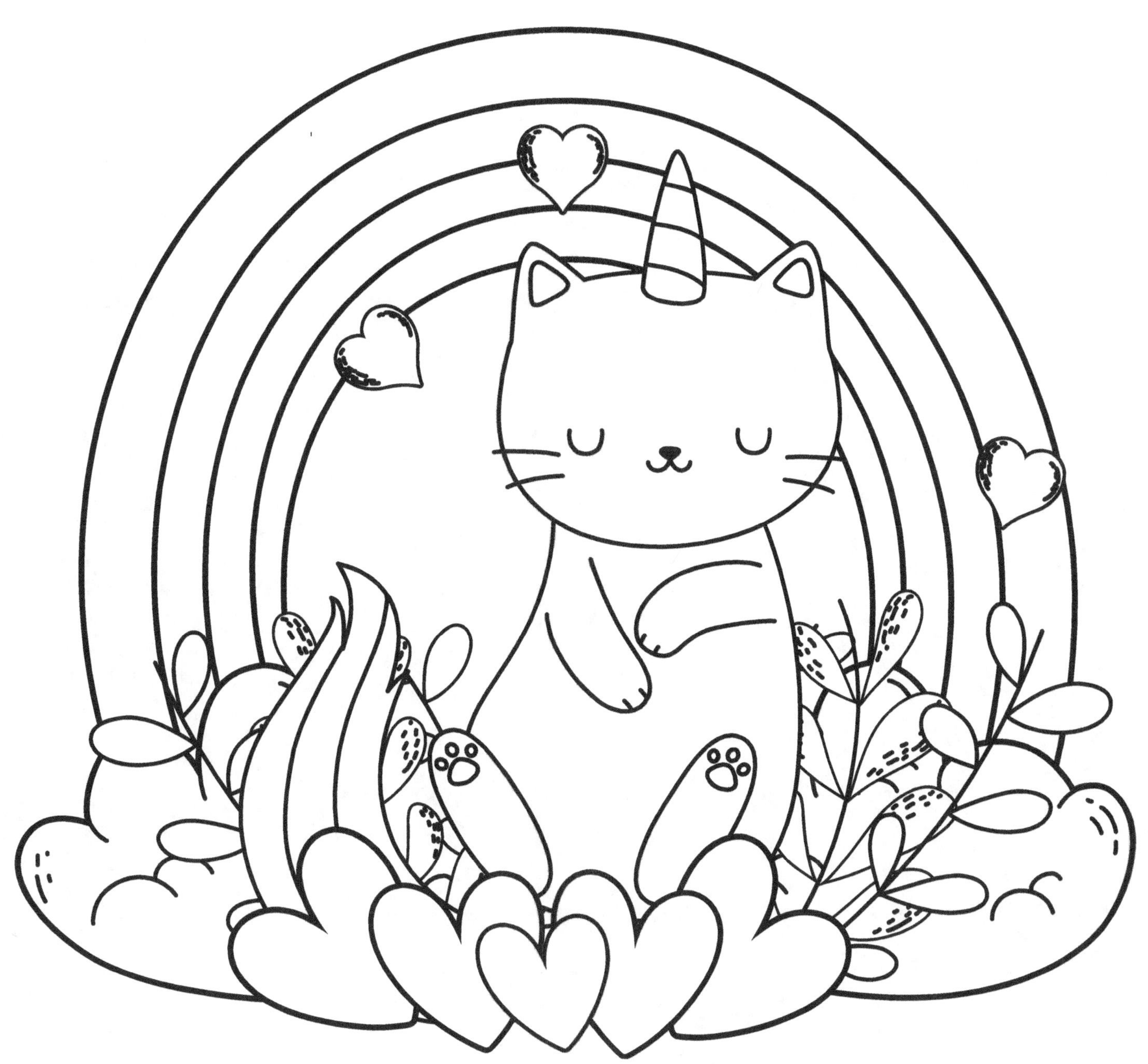

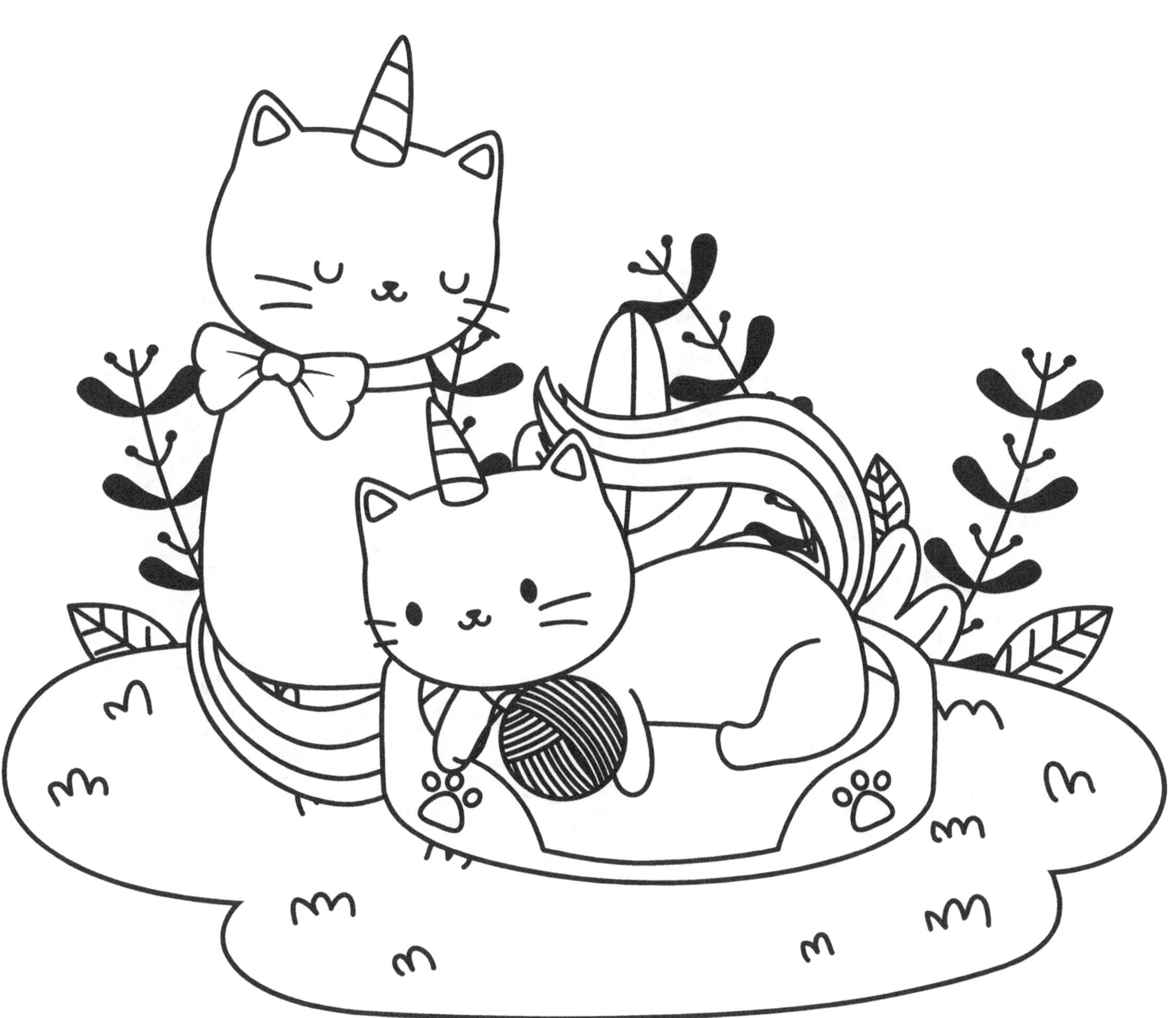

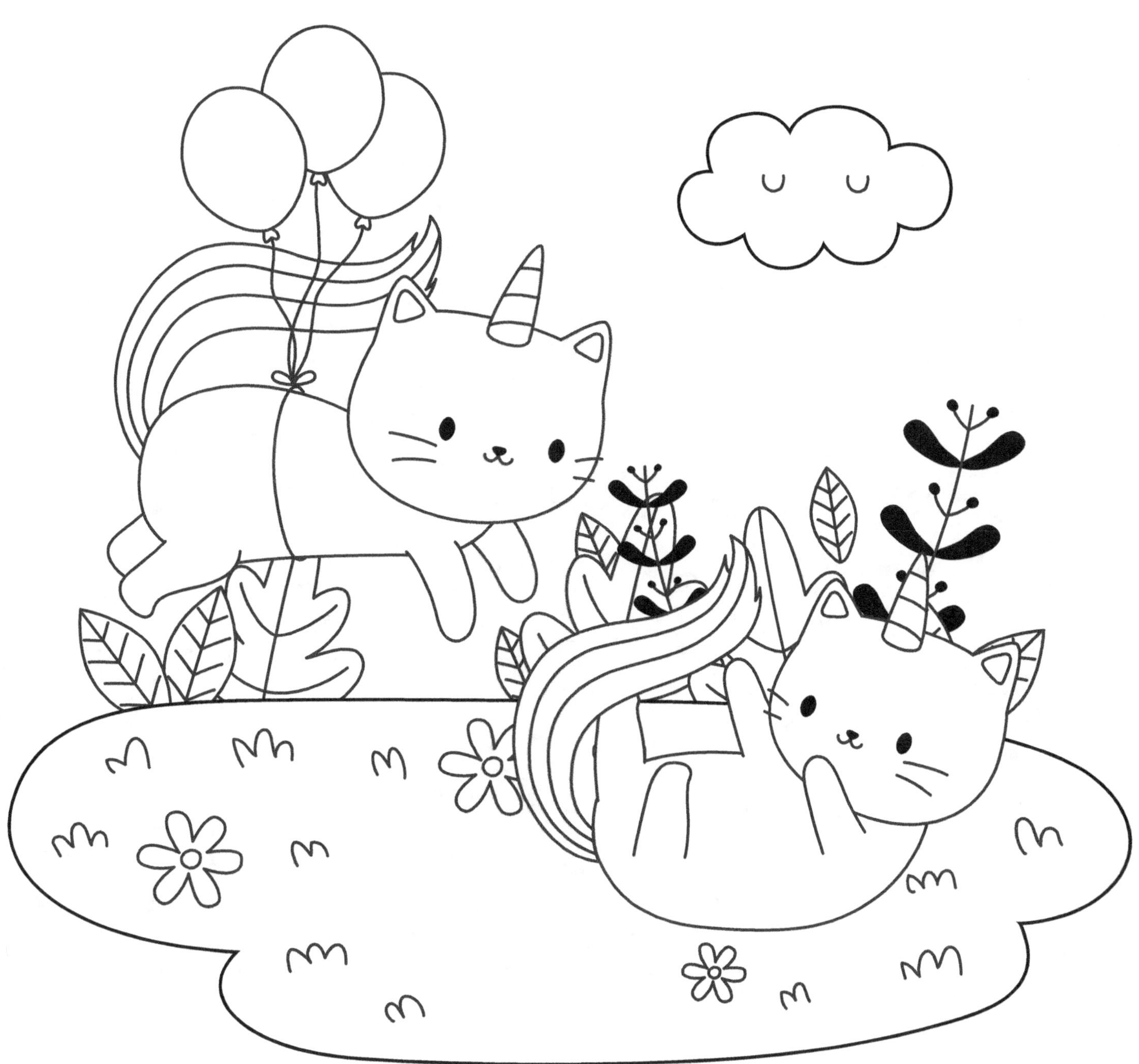

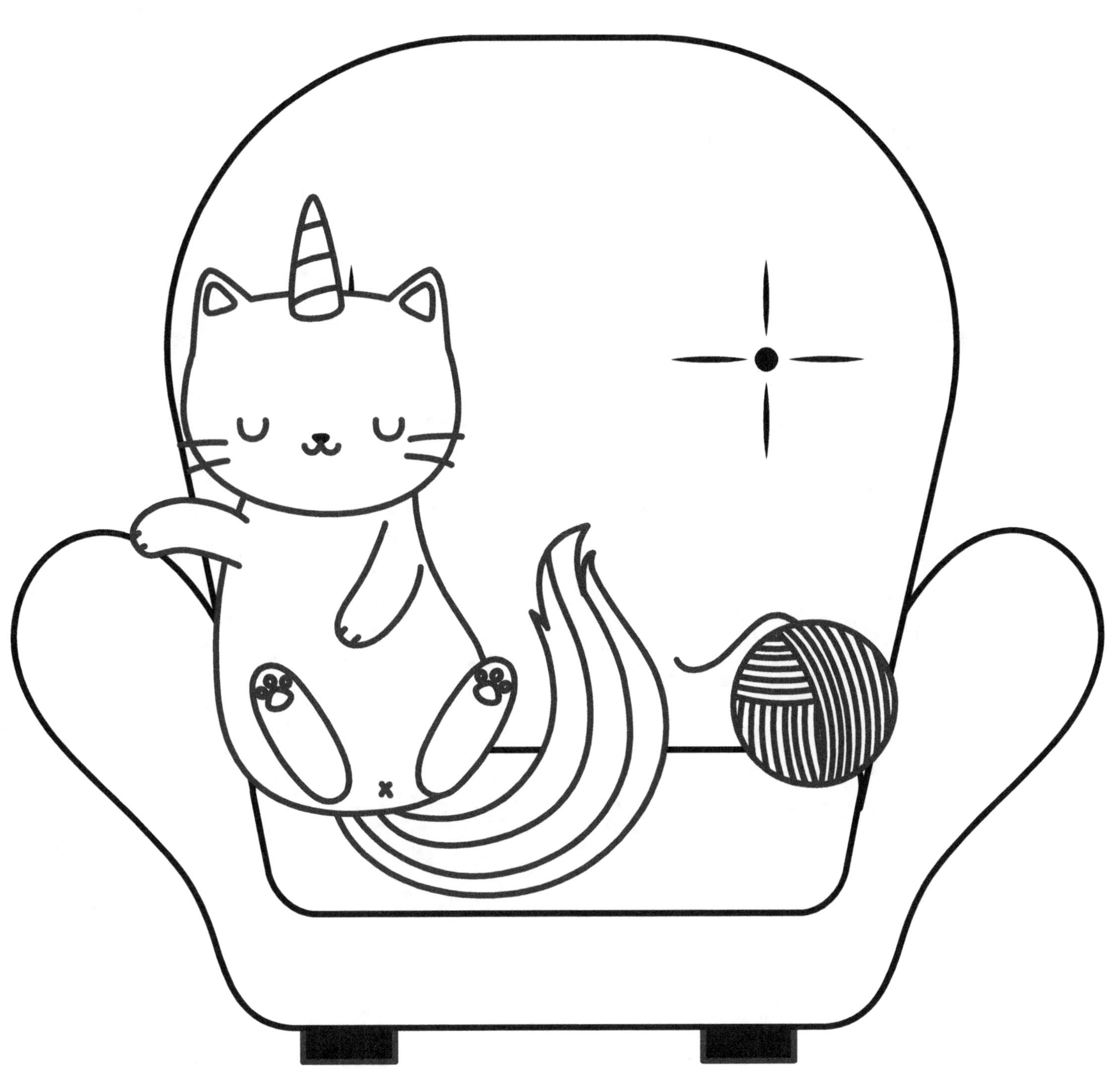

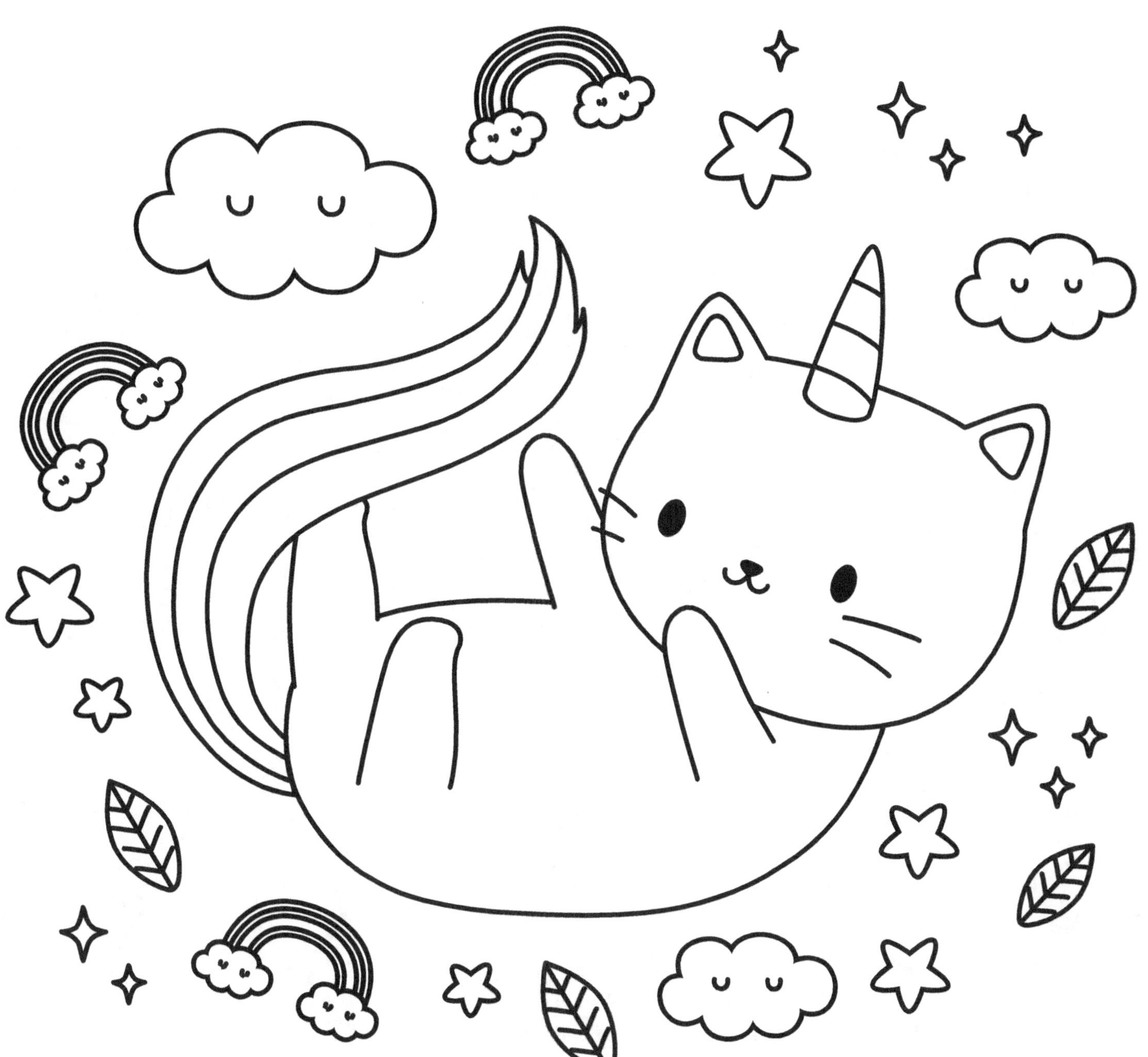

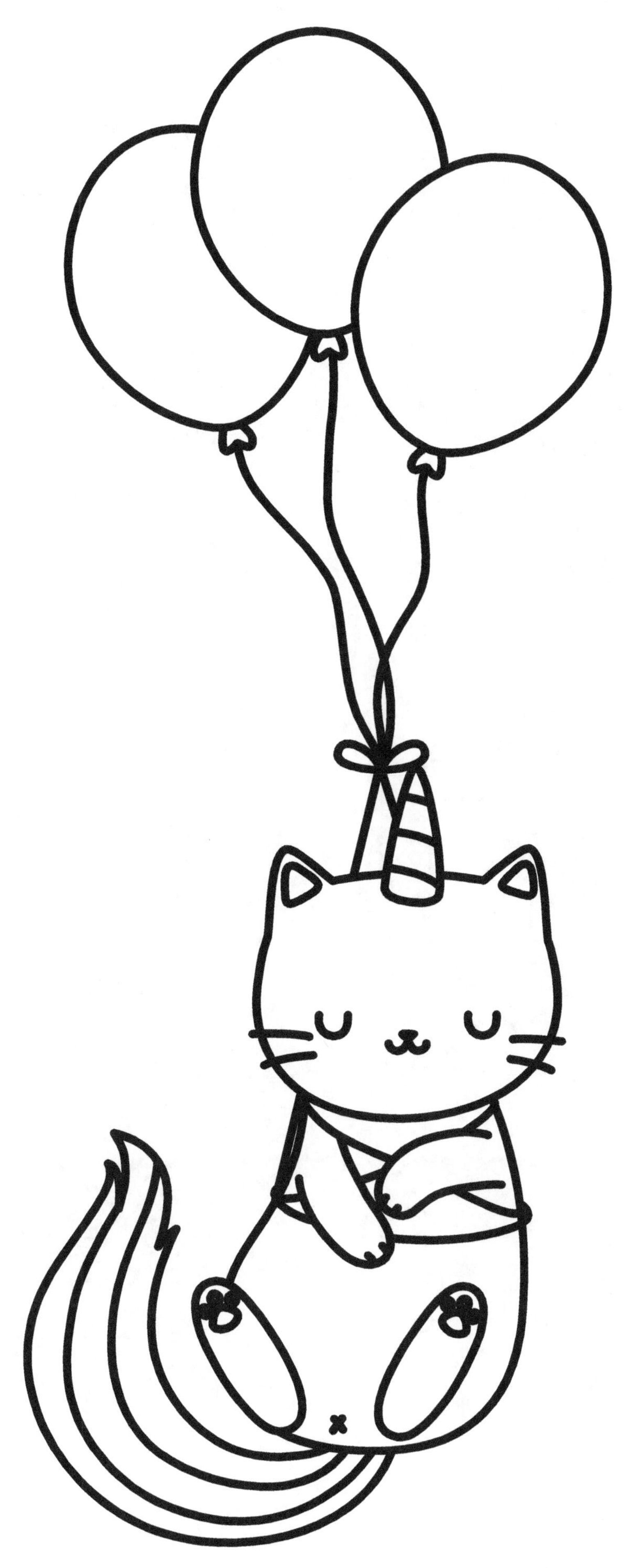

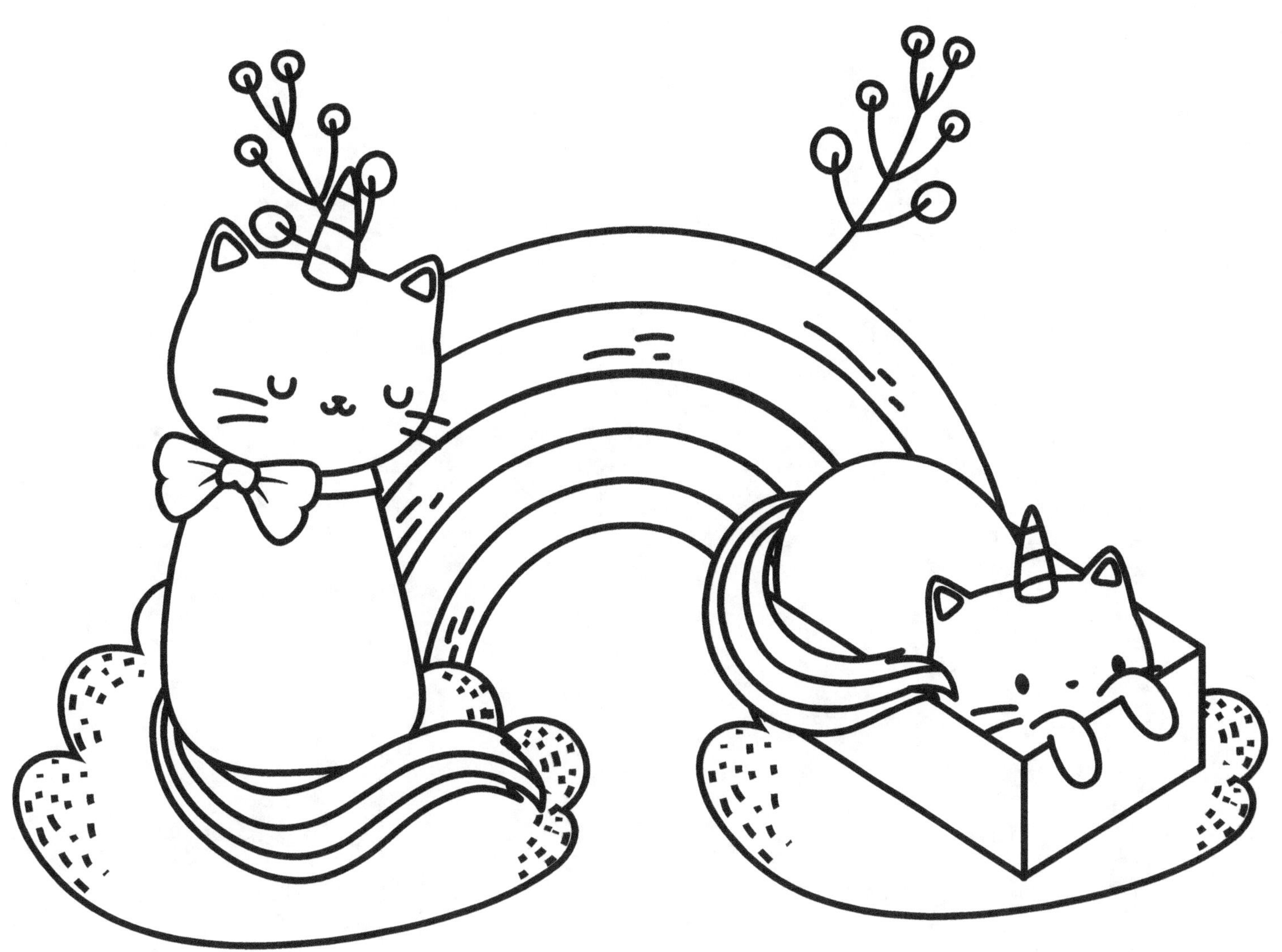

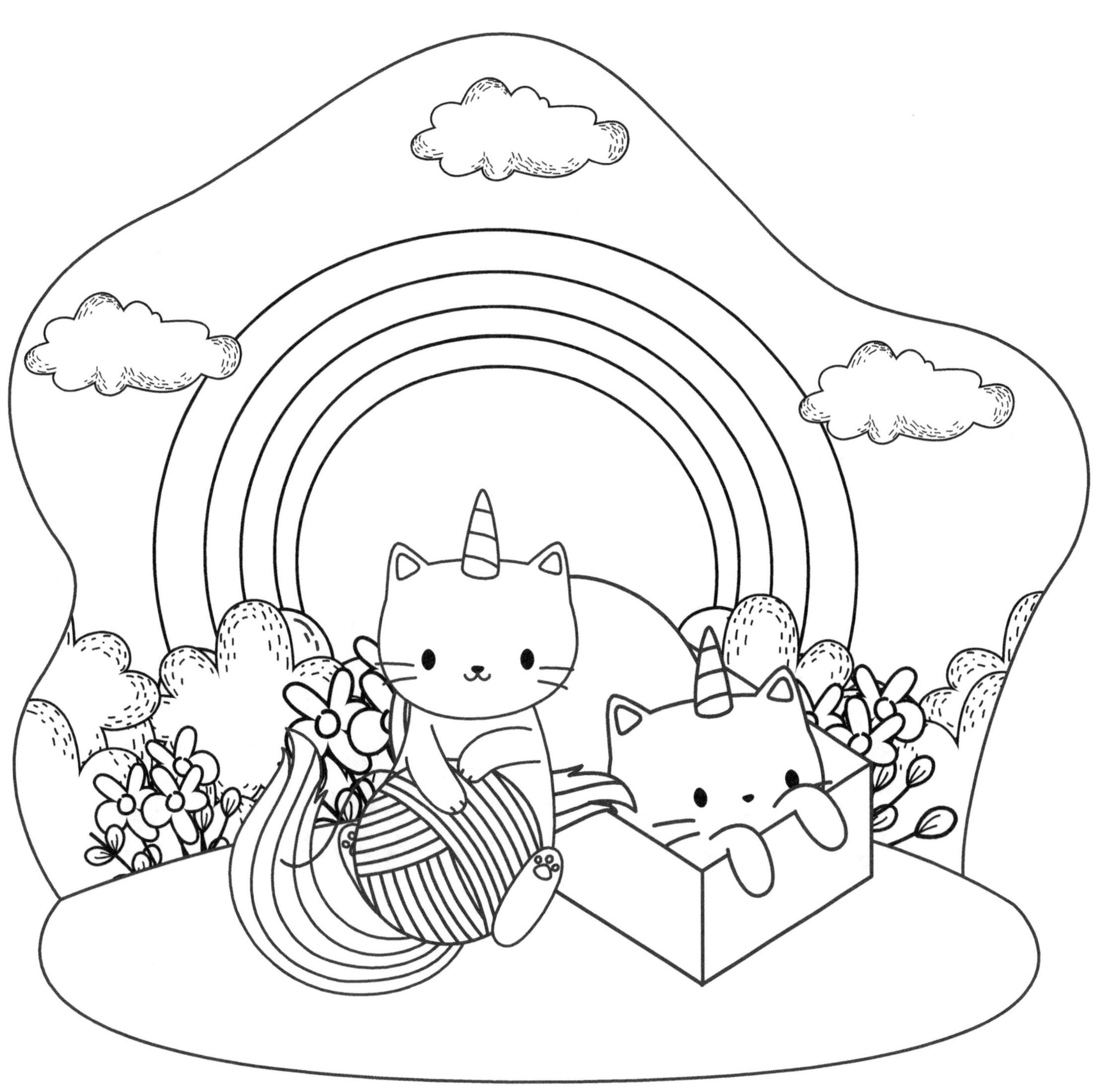

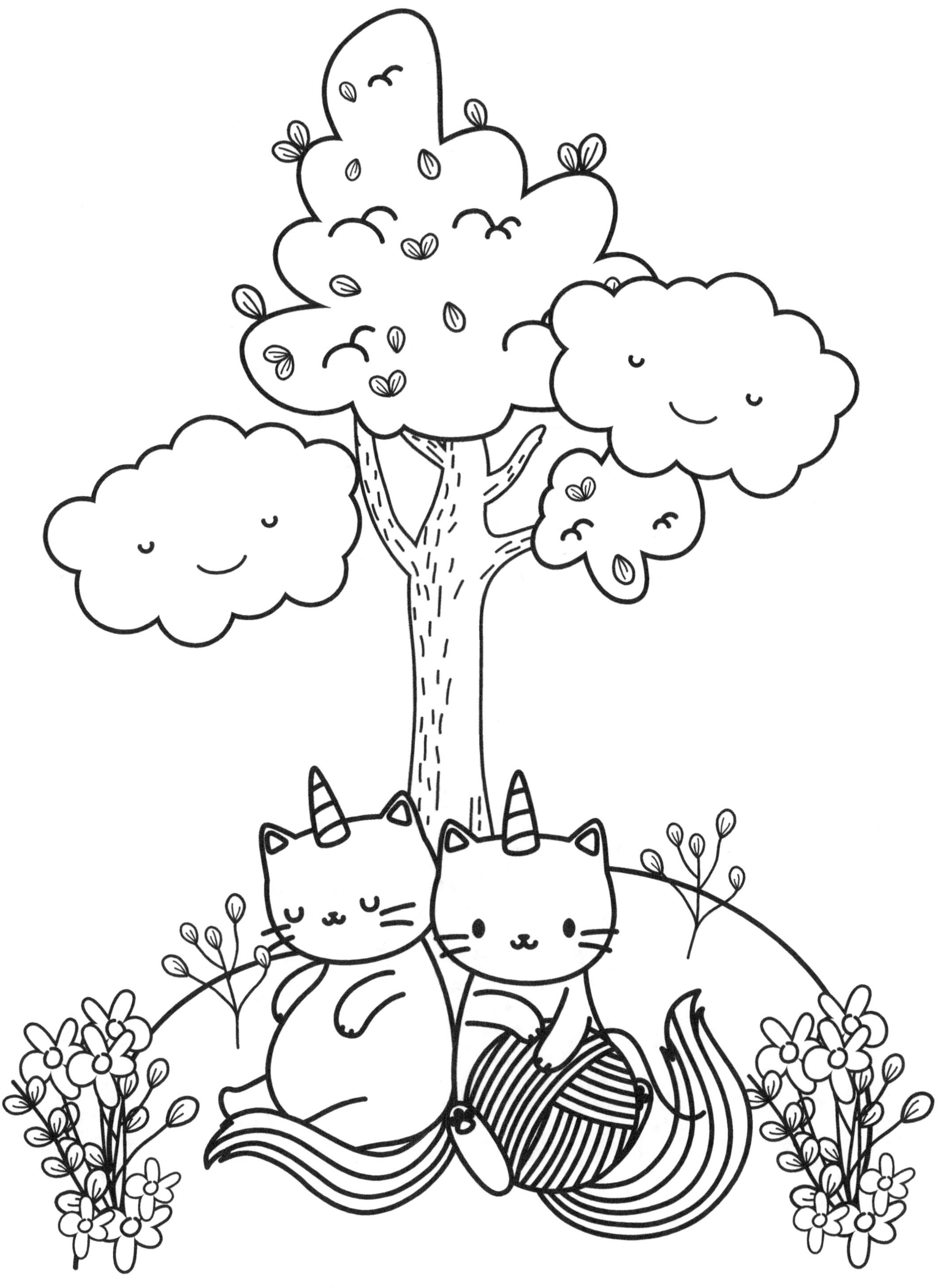

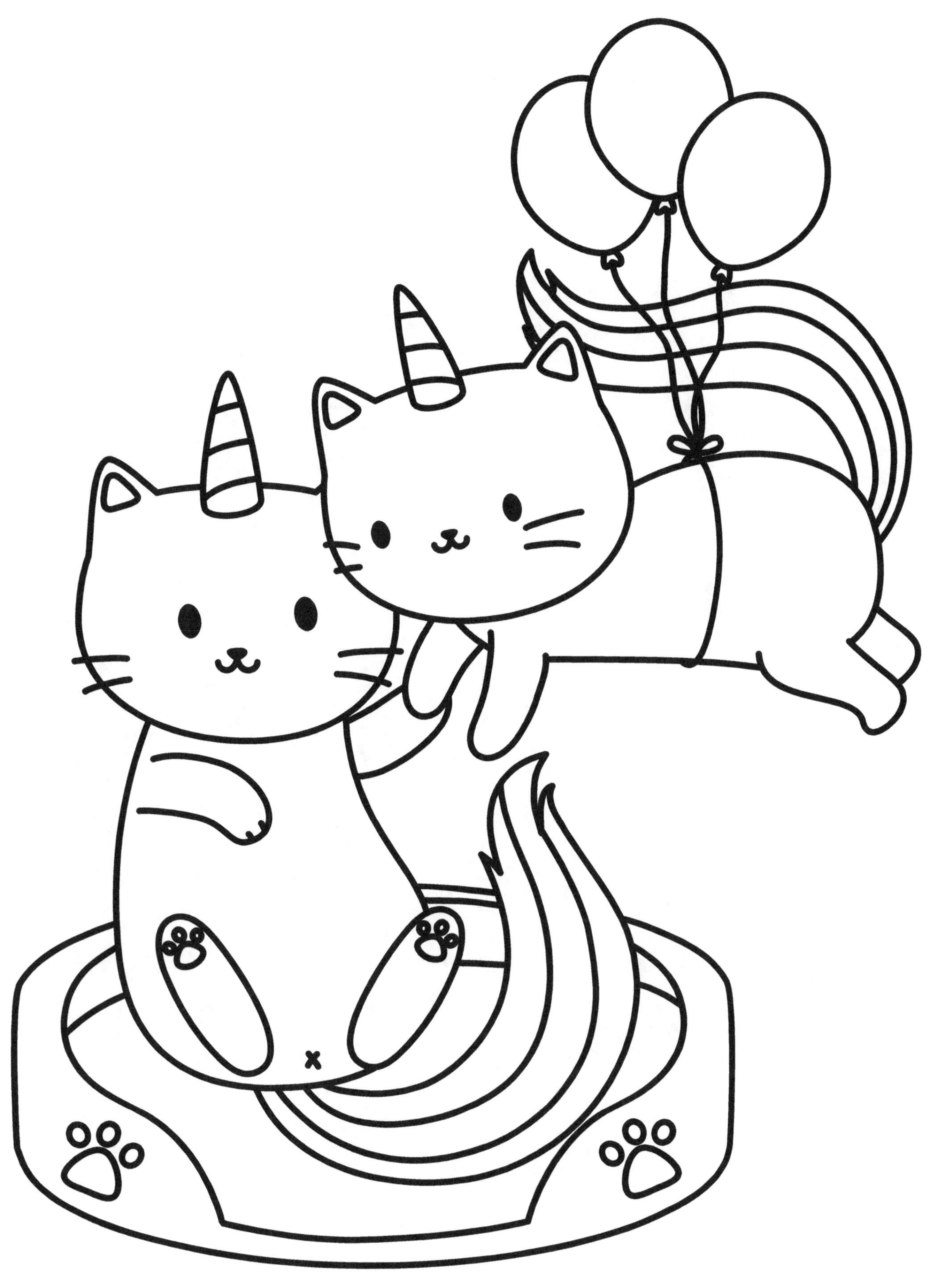

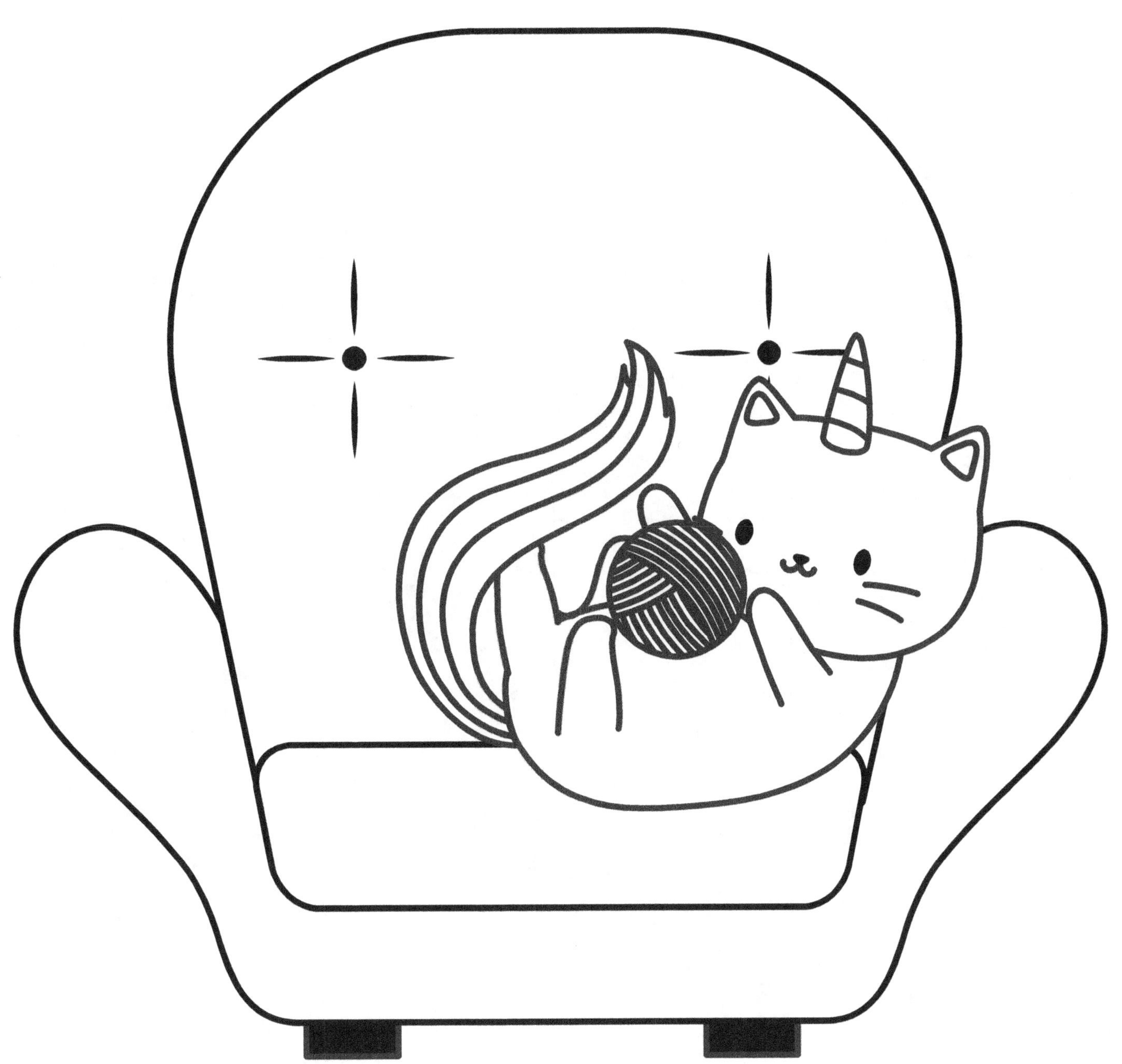

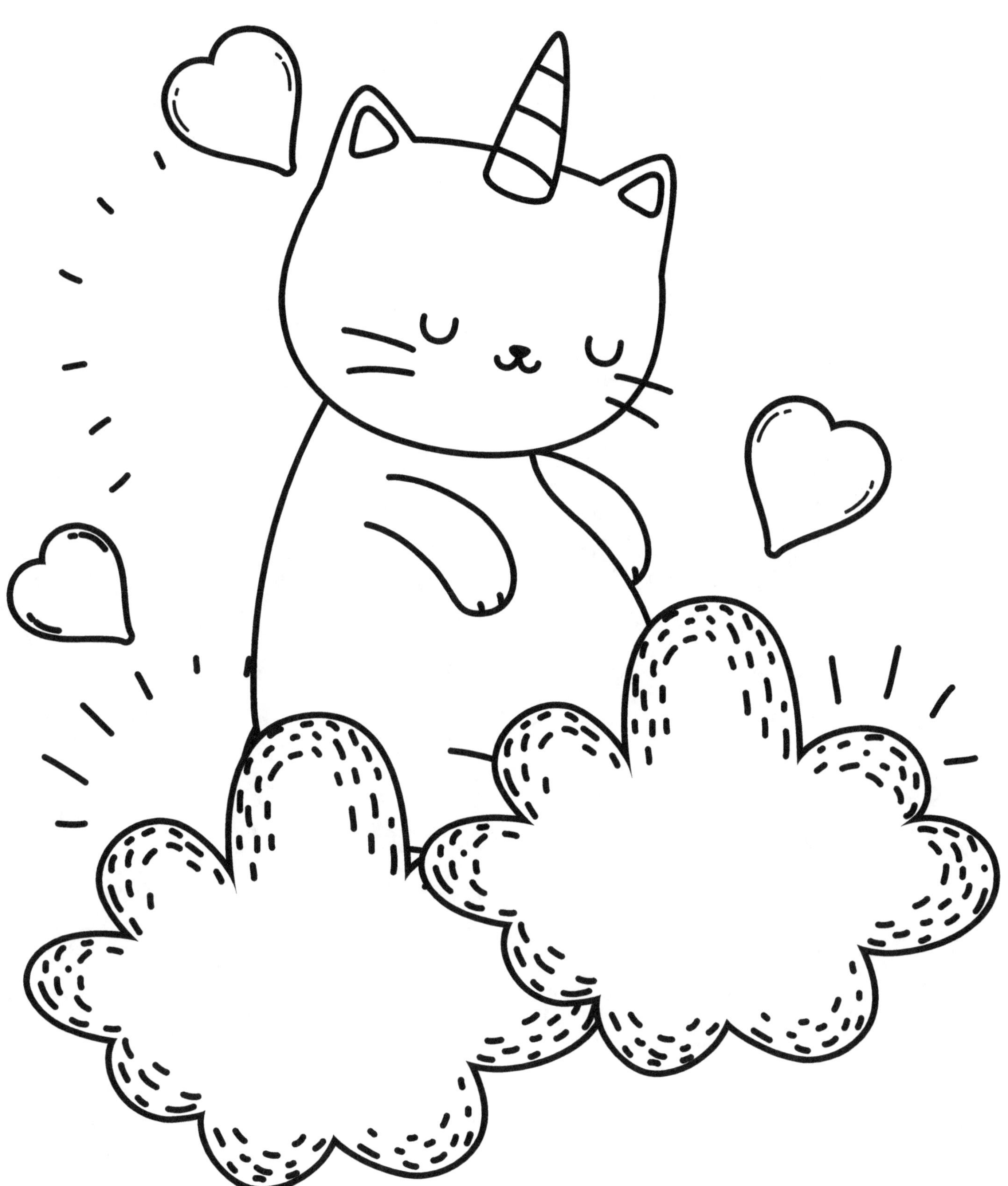

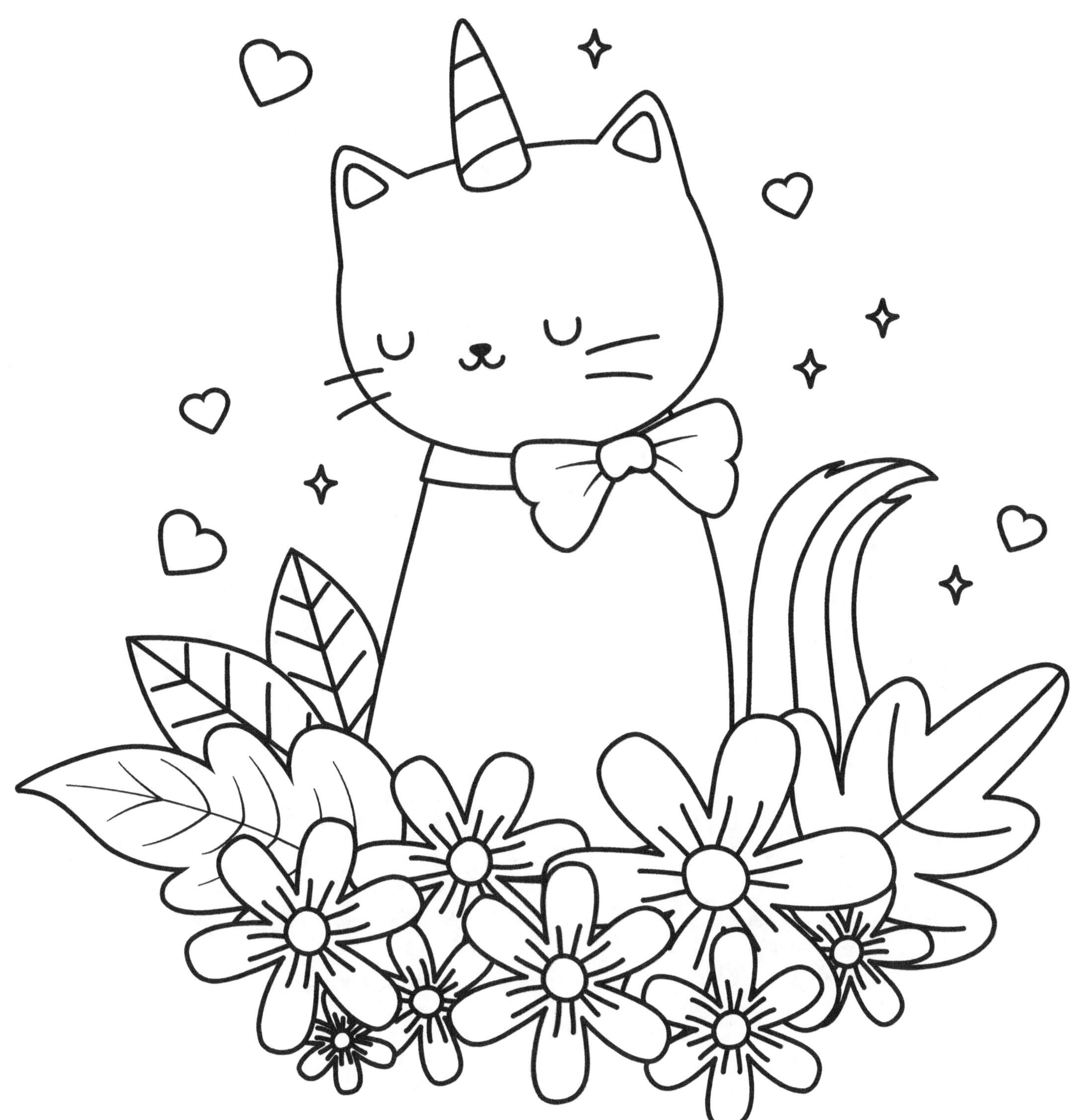

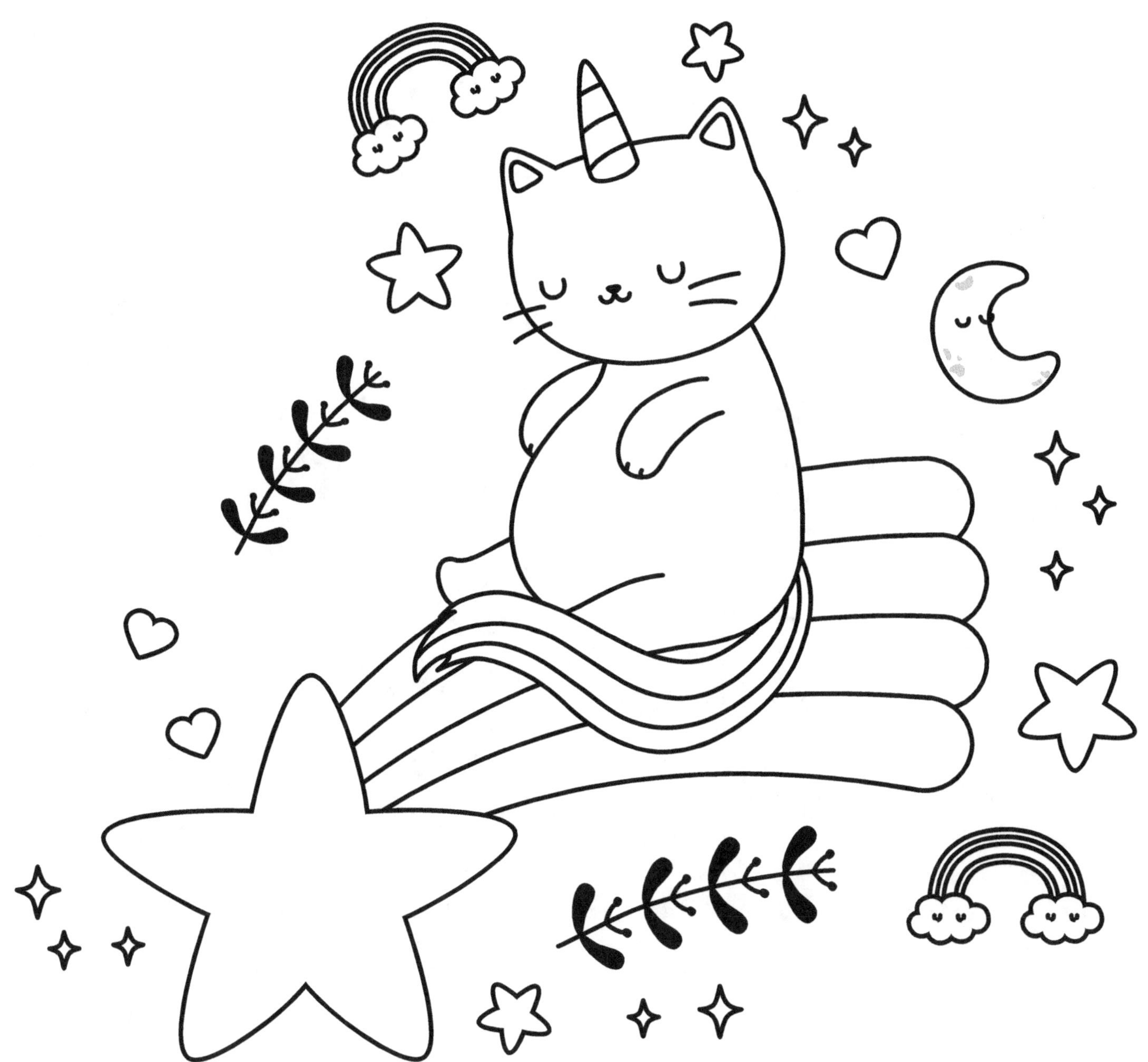

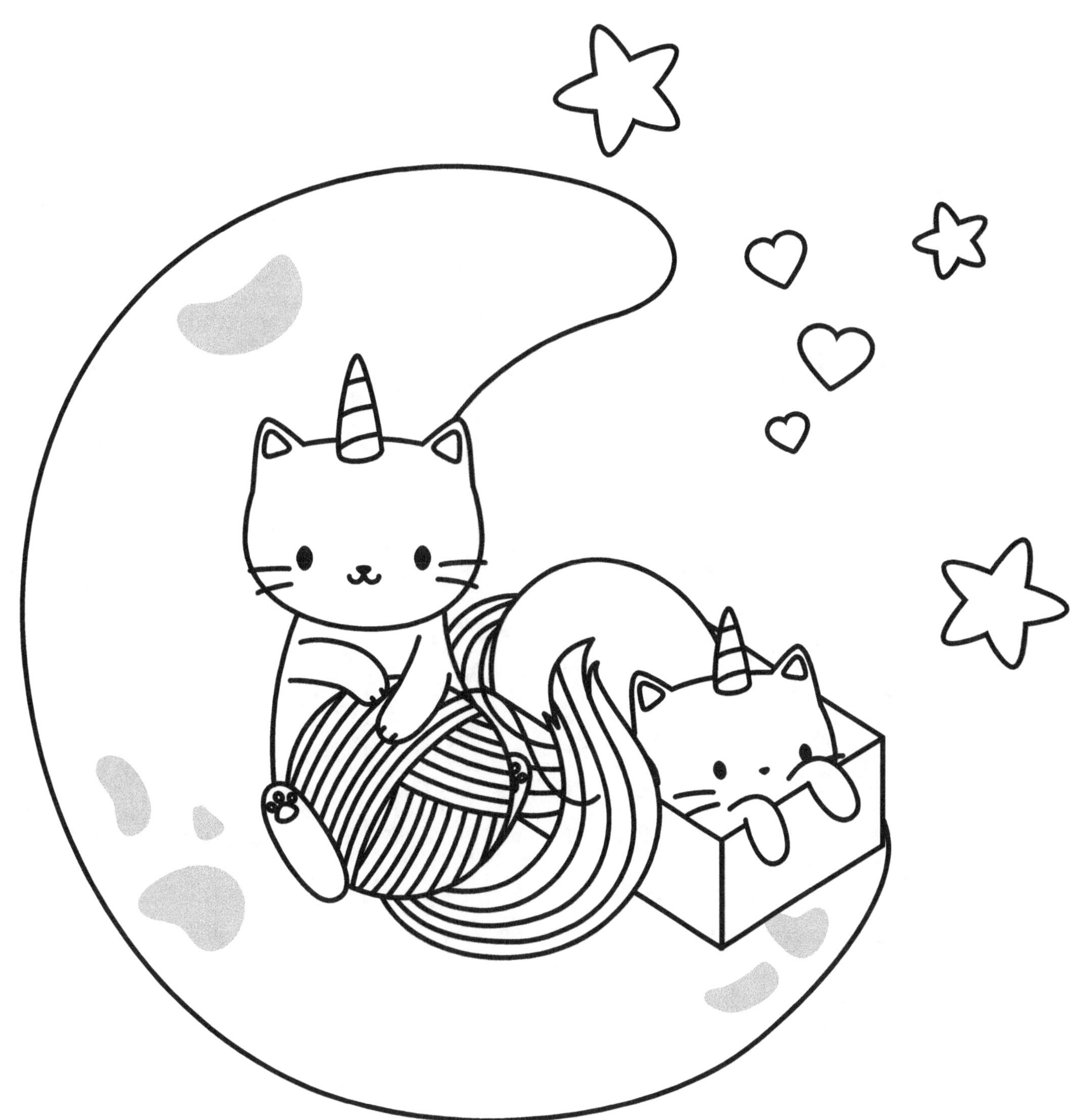

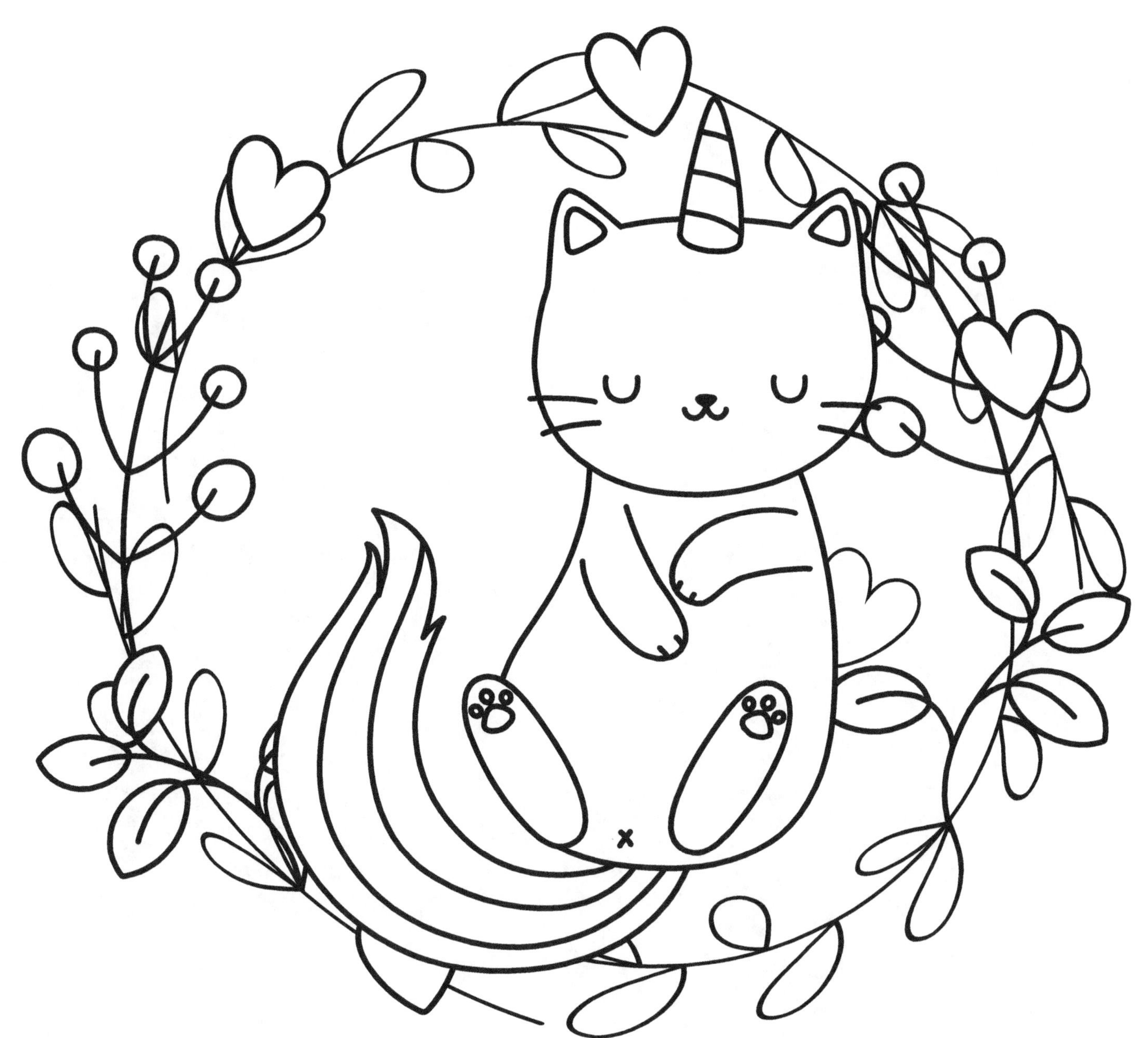

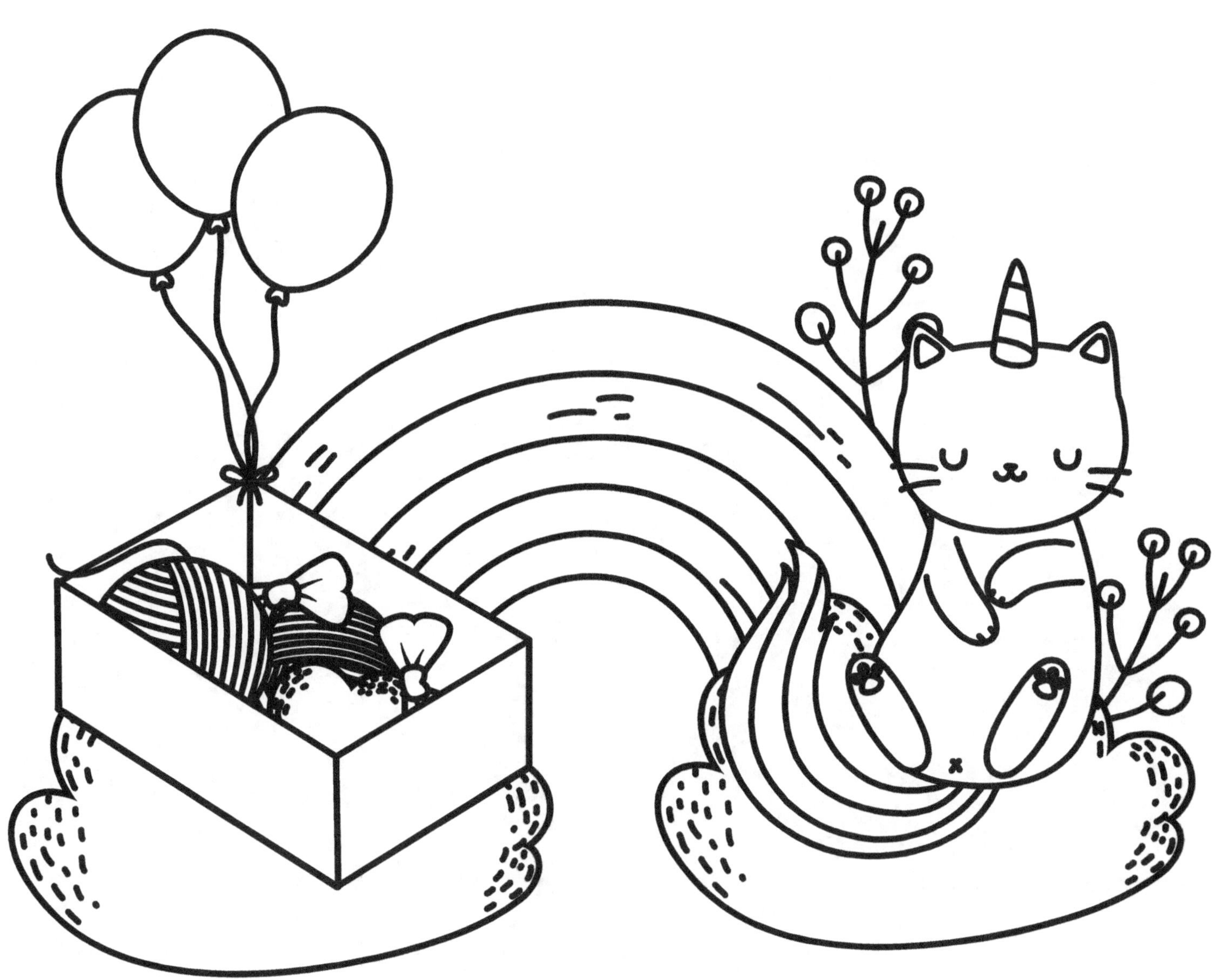

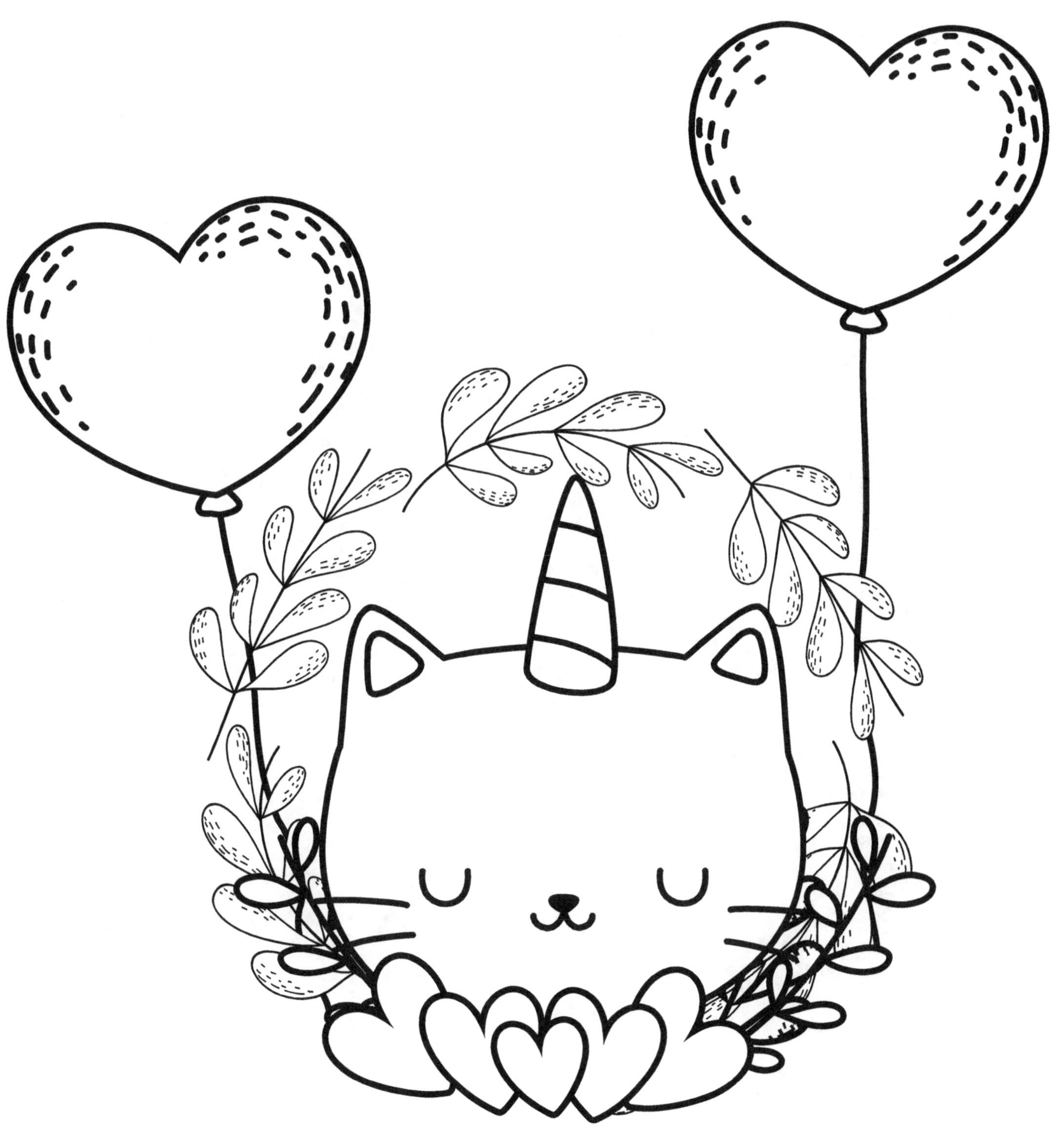

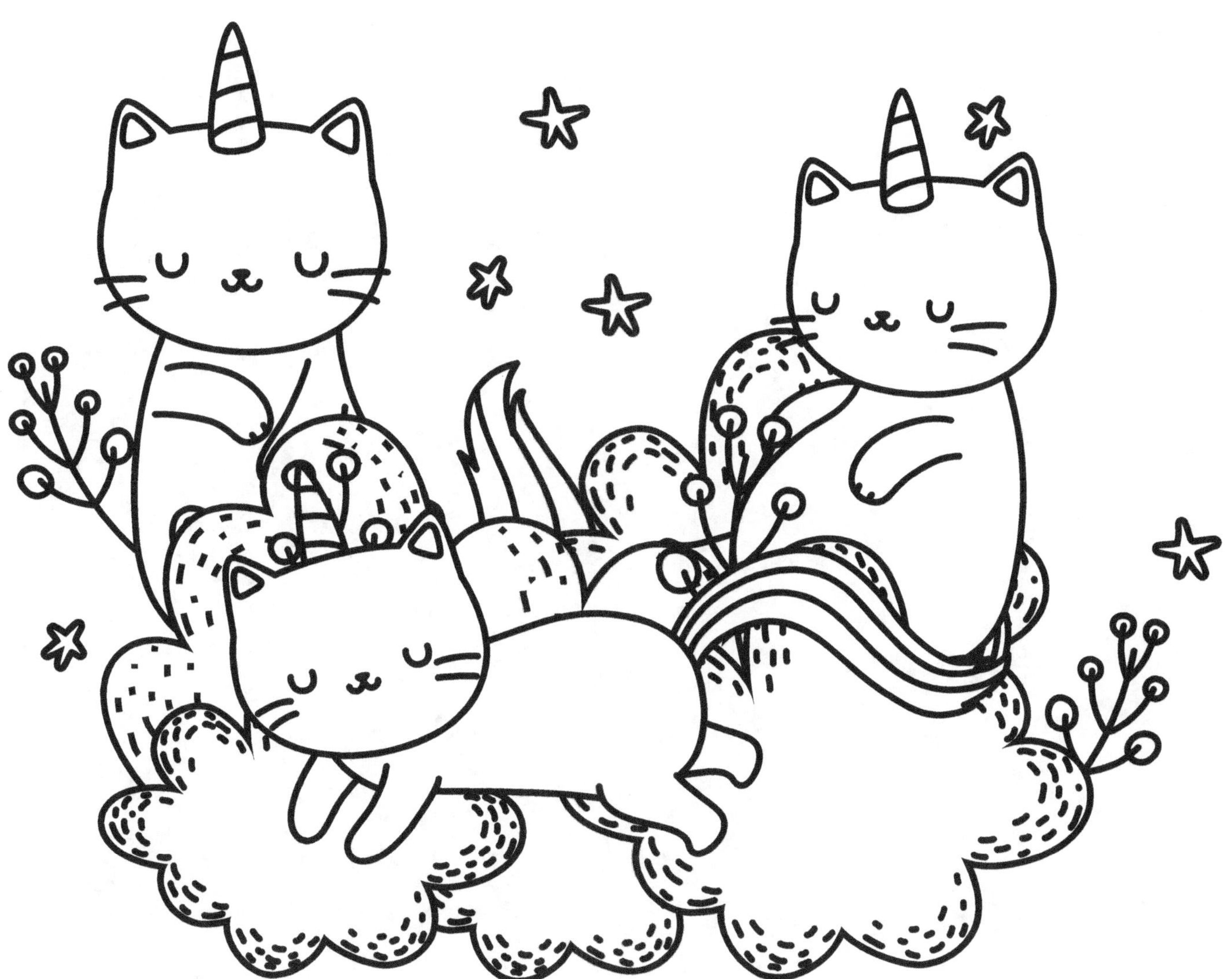

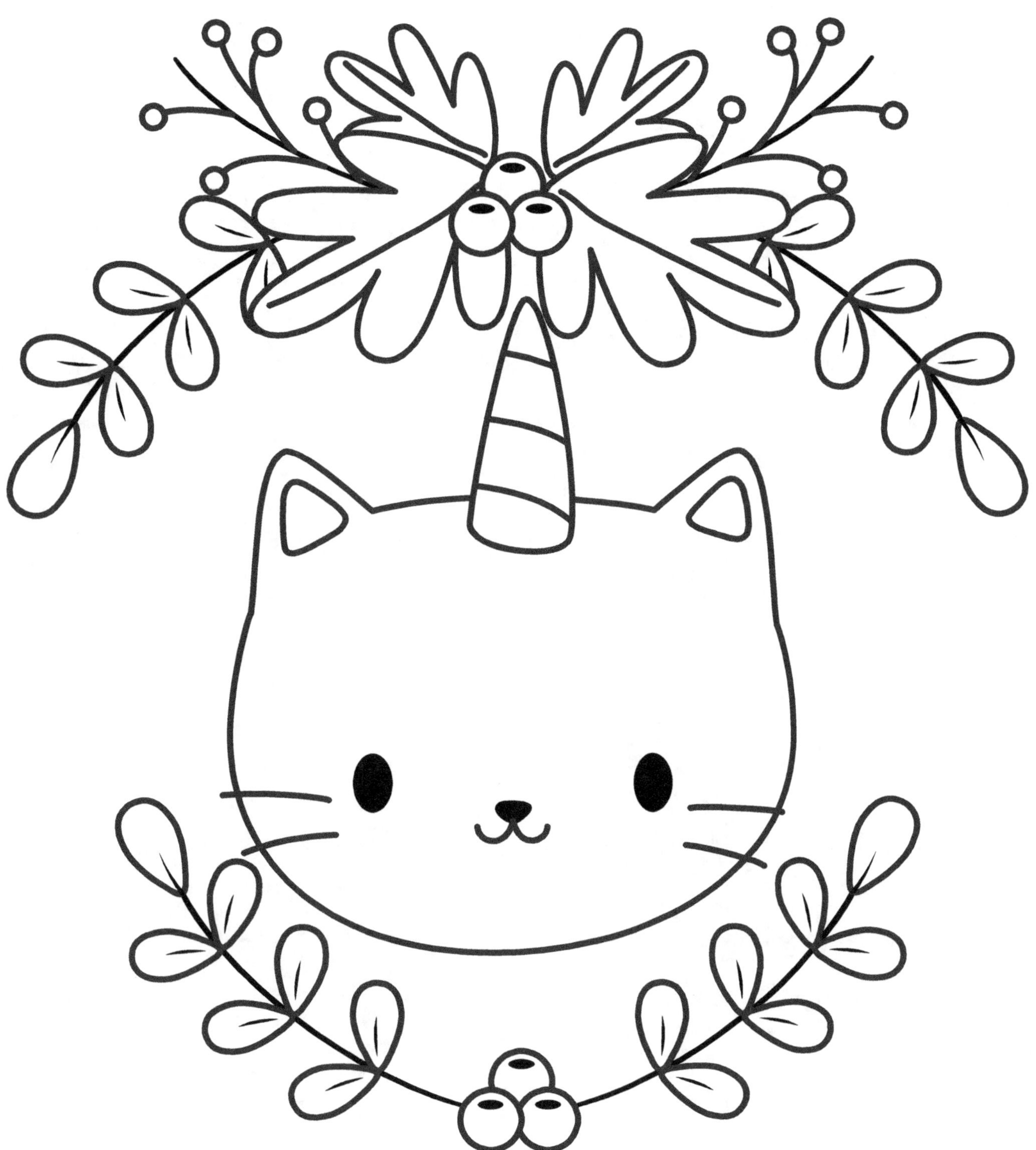

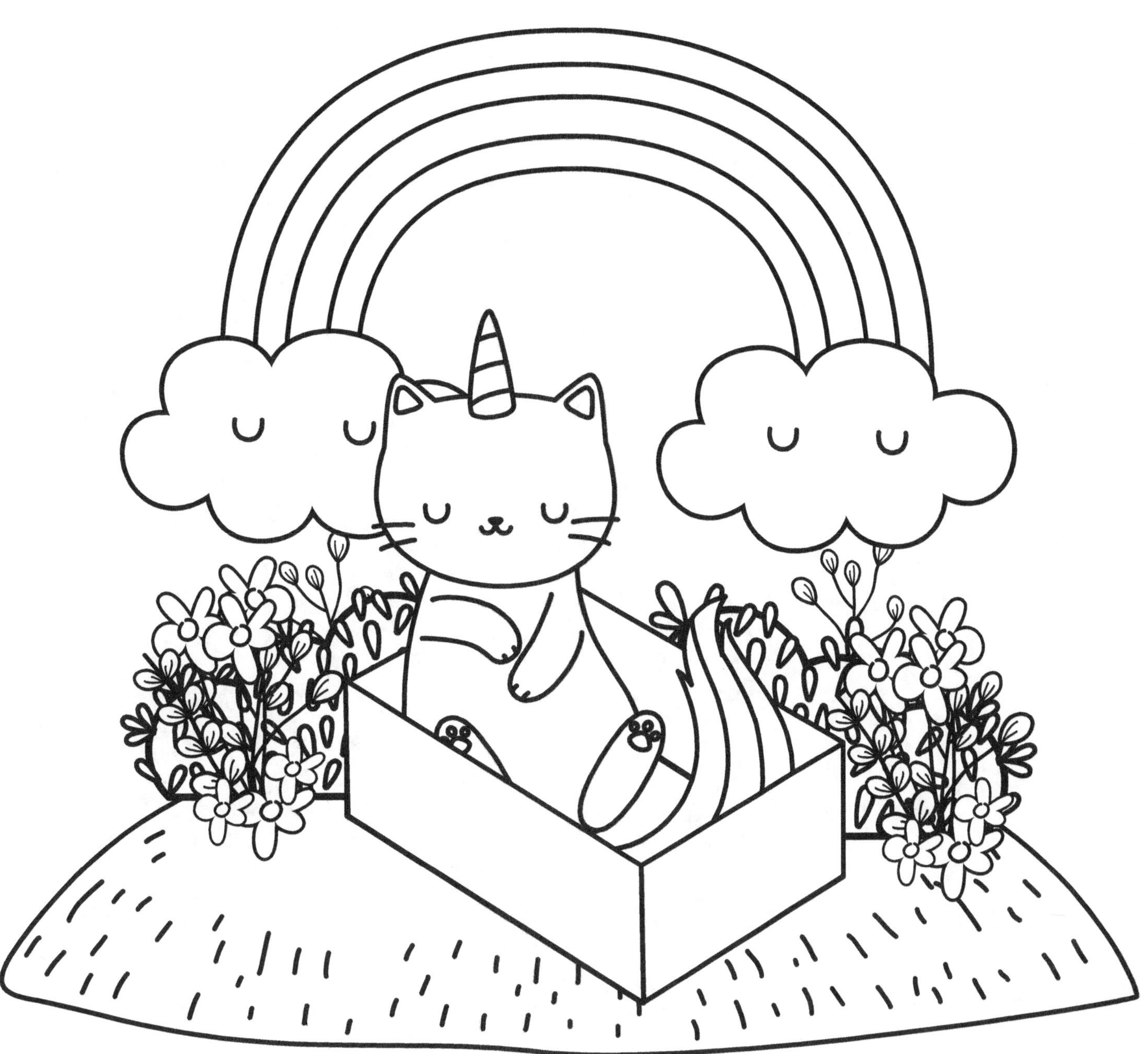

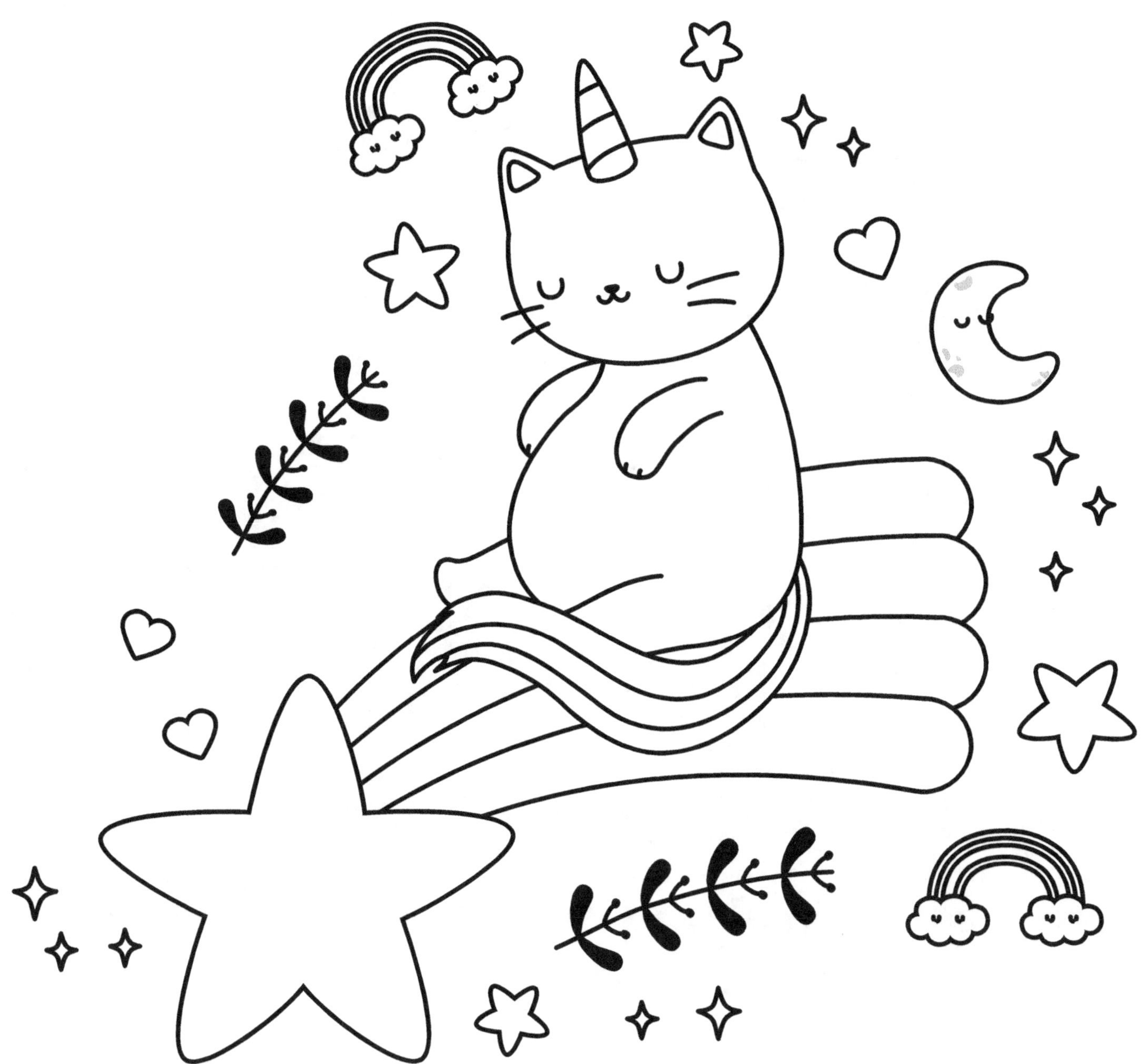

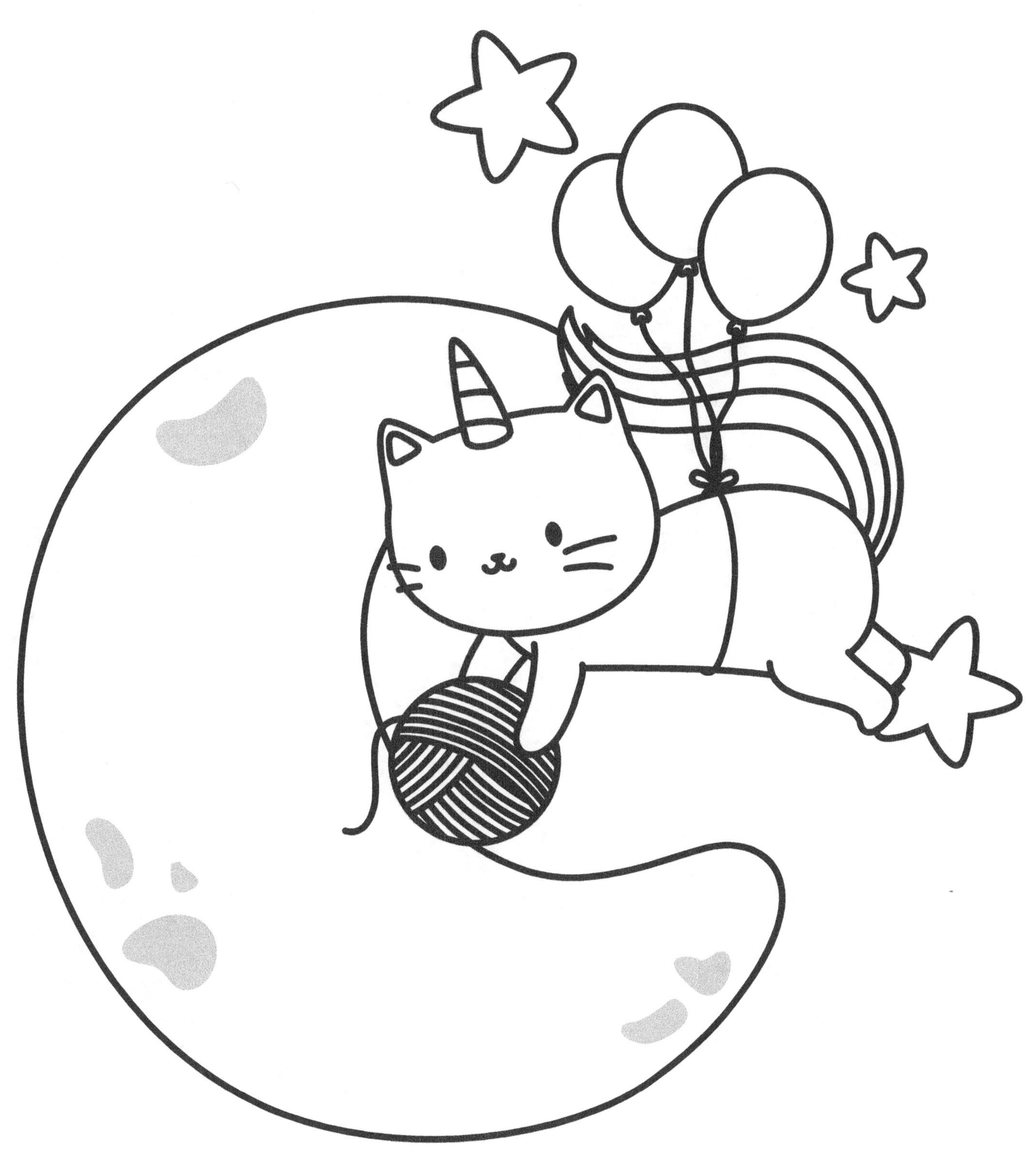

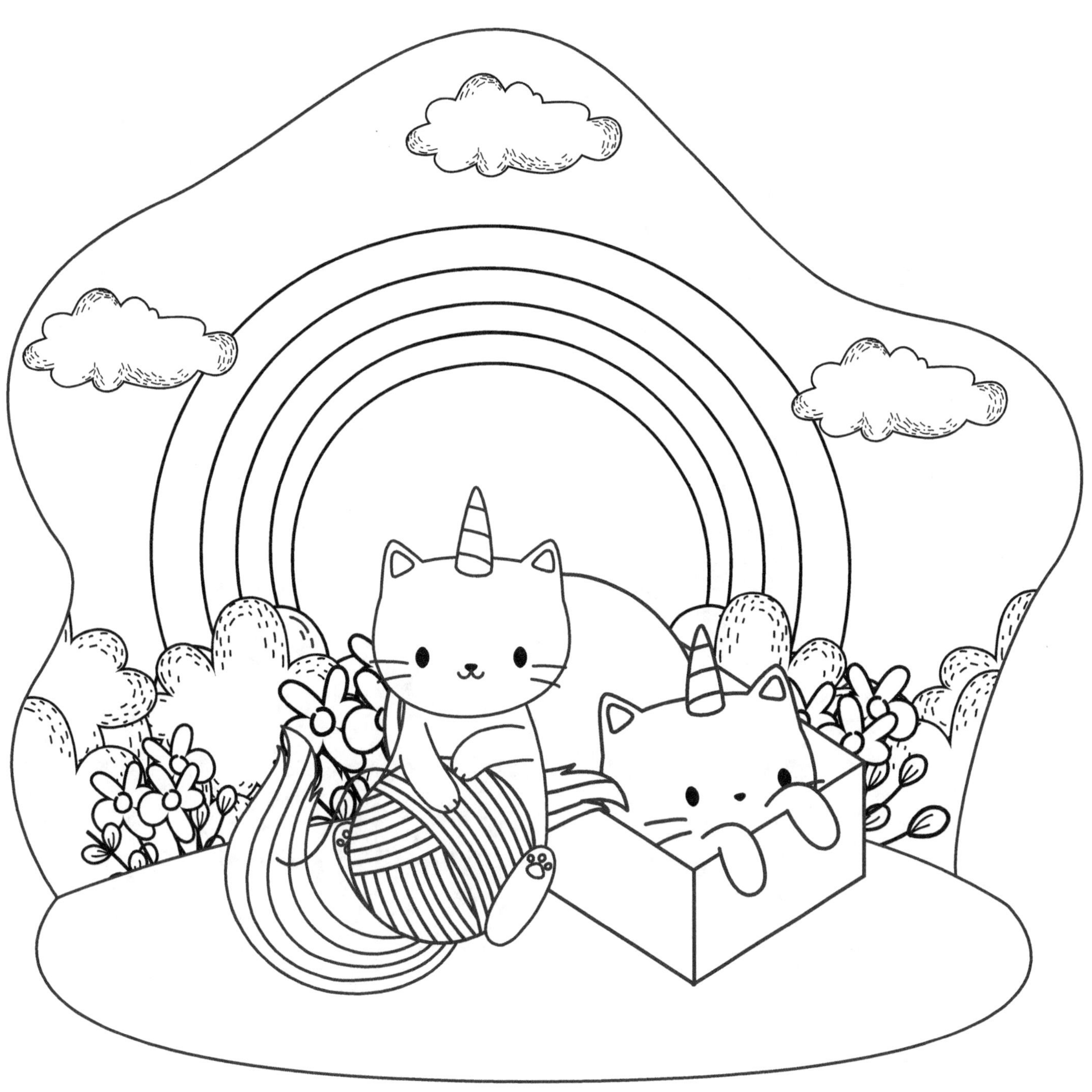

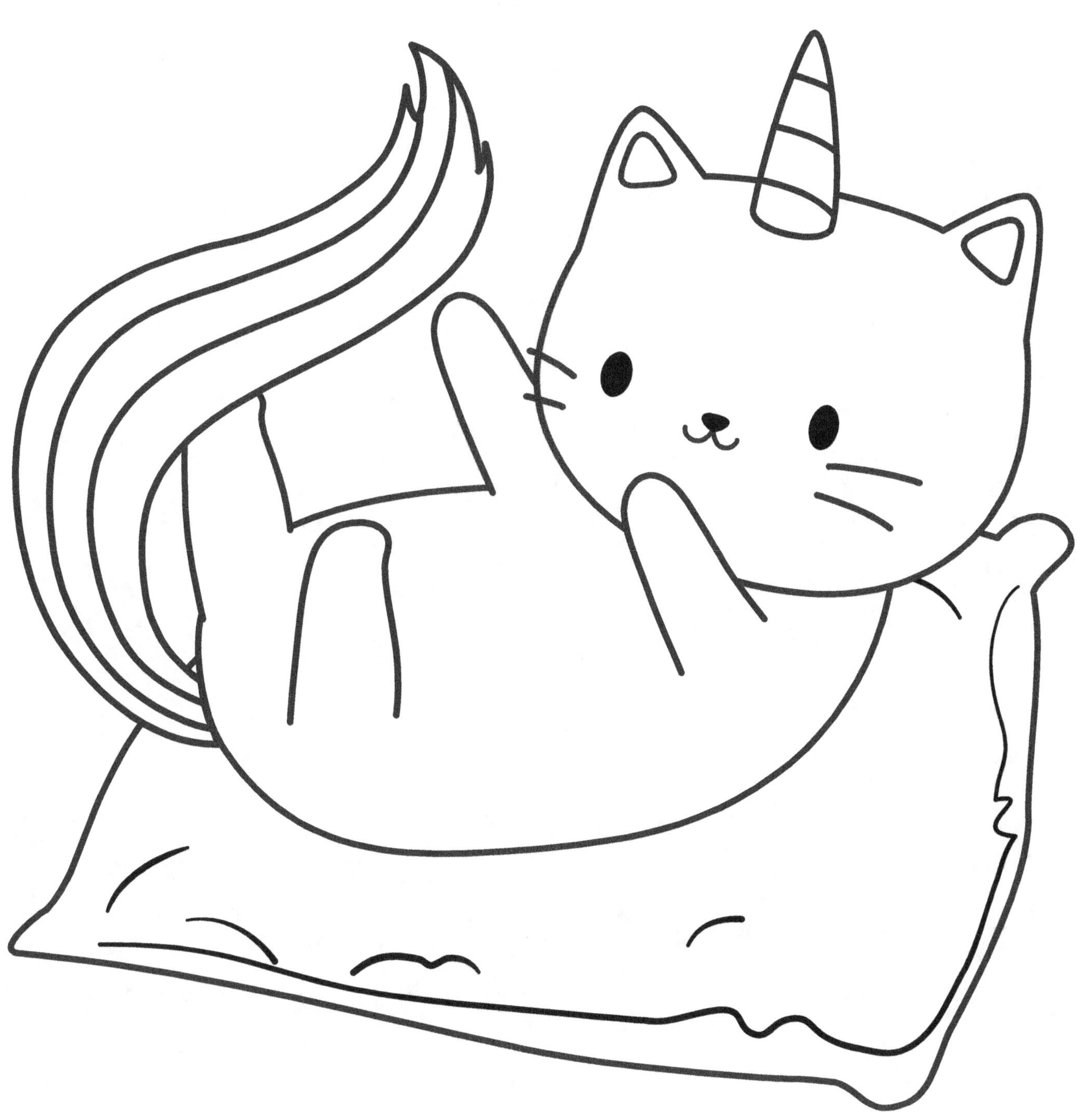

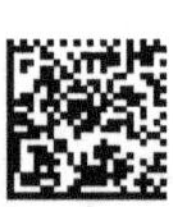

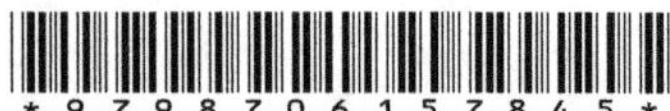
9 798706 157845